YOUR INVITATION TO GROW ORCHIDS

Orchid growing is the most fascinating hobby in the world.

YOU CAN GROW ORCHIDS. This book tells you how.

This book is for you if you know little or nothing about orchids and have only a few plants, or if you do not have your first plant yet. It is for you if you have a little knowledge and want more.

It is for you if you are a dirt gardener who likes to watch things grow, or an indoor gardener who wants to live with plants and enjoy exotic flowers the year-round.

Why Grow Orchids?

FOR FUN. The orchid family is the most interesting plant family of all, and one of the largest. It spreads all over the world. The flowers are the most highly developed of all flowers. It is a challenging hobby in which your whole family can participate, each with his own special interest.

FOR FLOWERS. You may think of corsage orchids, flowers that are purple, white, pink or yellow in the typical shape. That is only the beginning. Orchid blooms come in soft pastel, bright green, rich gold, red, yellow, dark mahogany, dazzling crimson, fuchsia and lavender-blue. There is every color except black. The all-black orchid is a myth.

Flower sizes run from pinheads to exhibition type hybrids, some almost a foot in width. Some flowers appear singly, some are produced in mammoth bouquets or lengthy sprays, some in succession on a stem. The shapes are astonishing. Some flowers look like butterflies, others like spiders, ballet dancers or hooded nuns. The flowers may be bizarre or beautiful. Take your pick.

There are different orchids which bloom at different seasons. By selecting plants with assorted schedules, you can have flowers almost continuously with only a dozen or more plants.

FOR RELAXATION. Orchids do take time. All plants take time and attention. Orchids are tough, and you can keep them alive with a minimum of care during your busy periods, providing you meet their basic needs.

In this age of stress, working with your orchids is as relaxing as time spent bicycling or sitting in a Jacuzzi. A few hours in the greenhouse with your orchids will do wonders for you, even at the end of a long, hard day. Working with plants relieves tensions and helps to solve personal problems.

FOR PEOPLE. Orchid people are interesting. Orchids are no longer just for the rich and famous. Most hobby growers are middle class working people all over the world. Some are executives. Others are professionals or TV stars. Some are blue collar workers. Many are retired people who find this hobby provides daily challenges. Whatever your career or social status, you will find congenial people with a common interest but diverse daily lives, and you will make lasting friends in the orchid fraternity. Orchid shows, orchid societies, orchid meetings and other activities offer an opportunity to get involved with other interesting people.

A Popular Hobby

A few wealthy people were growing orchids 150 years ago. But after the middle of this century, orchids became popular with everybody. Until then plants were expensive, equipment was scarce and information was hard to acquire. Those of us who have been orchid hobbyists for 40 years or more are pioneers. Now there are hobby growers by the thousands.

Four things have contributed to the astonishing increase in orchid growing by amateurs in recent times.

One factor is mass production of orchid plants. This was brought about by the discovery in 1922 of a better method of germinating orchid seed. As a result, commercial growers were able to produce more plants than they needed for cut flowers. Mass production brought prices down and made plants more available. Further, recent developments in cloning plants have resulted in mass production of fine or scarce varieties, likewise improving availability while reducing prices. Now potted, blooming orchid plants may be comparable in price to other blooming potted plants.

Another point was development of mass production of small greenhouses. Orchids that once were grown only on large estates have now moved to the suburbs. A small greenhouse may cost less than a boat or a swimming pool to buy and maintain. Prefabricated greenhouses are available from a number of companies. Plants are "at home" hobbies that provide entertainment in any weather and at any hour of the day or night.

But not everybody has a greenhouse. Many hobbyists grow orchids in high rise condominiums, city apartments, or home basements under artificial lights. In temperate climates plants grow out of doors in mild weather. Cymbidiums are favored landscape plants in California gardens.

Another contributing factor to the interest in orchid growing is the ever-increasing interest in plants of all kinds. We accept plants as necessary

(Top) Phalaenopsis are called "moth orchids." They bloom on long sprays and the flowers may last for several weeks.

(Lower) Slipper orchids of the genus Paphiopedilum are easy to recognize because the lip is shaped like the toe of a shoe.

items in interior decorating in homes and businesses. Note the new office buildings and hotels that have lavish indoor gardens. Examine any high quality magazine that pictures glamorous interiors in ads or editorial matter and note the potted plants, many of which are blooming orchids right in their own pots or displayed in cache pots. Orchid flowers may stay fresh and pretty for a week, even several weeks, so they are long lasting flowers for the house.

And fourth, the increased availability of information. People share knowledge with friends. Orchid societies on local, regional and national levels conduct shows, seminars, tours. There are a number of fine orchid magazines to help you, premier of which is the monthly American Orchid Society Bulletin.

This book and its sequels are among many current books for hobby growers. And there is a wealth of information in print about orchids. Many of the books of a century ago are color plate classics with gorgeous illustrations, but there are old and new books about culture, native orchids of many countries, scientific advancements, hybrids, and other aspects of orchid growing.

Join the Orchid Fraternity

This is your invitation to join the orchid fraternity. You need three qualifications: a genuine interest in these flowers and plants, a willingness to learn more, and a devotion to providing your plants with proper care so they grow and bloom.

Orchid growing is an enchanting hobby and a challenge. If you live to be a hundred, you won't begin to see all the orchids already in existence and new ones are blooming every day. Every grower has his own techniques for growing his plants, and you need to determine what works best for you and your plants. There is always something to learn, as new developments lead you on.

A Bit of Advice

You must understand that orchids do have certain requirements and you must tend to their needs. Survival isn't enough. You want your plants to grow to perfection and produce their finest flowers.

Begin with blooming size plants that are suitable for the environment and care you can give them. Do not start with small seedlings, which are babies and need extra attention, and do not begin with newly imported plants that must be reestablished. Buy established mature plants in bloom so you can see what you are getting, and when you learn to care for them, you may wish to go into seedlings or small mericlones.

Always buy your plants from reliable, established nurseries. Plants should look healthy, have active roots, and show no evidence of pests or diseases. Beware of bargains until you know what really is a bargain. There are lots of really good plants available for reasonable prices.

CHAPTER I

THE FLOWERS

Orchids are highly developed flowers. They take on many different shapes, sizes and colors but the basic structure is the same whether it is a bulldog paphiopedilum, a butterfly oncidium or a spidery brassia.

There are six segments: three sepals and three petals on each flower. On every orchid one petal is different. This is the distinguishing feature.

SEPALS: On most garden flowers the sepals are rather inconspicuous. They are the outermost whorl of the flower. Sepals protect the delicate inner parts of the flower while it is developing. On a rose the sepals are the little green triangles that cover the bud when it is first formed, but they do not enlarge with it. When the rose opens, the petals are colored, but the sepals are still small and green and underneath the outer petals. Conversely, on a tulip, sepals are colorful and resemble petals.

On an orchid the sepals are included in the showy part of the flower. When the flower is a closed bud, the three sepals form the outer covering and the petals, though usually larger, are curled up inside.

When the orchid flower opens it appears to have six petals, but three of them are sepals, usually the same color as the two horizontal petals but perhaps narrower. They alternate with the petals in the flower design, but on examination of the back of a flower you will see that the sepals are lower on the stem.

PETALS: Of the three petals on an orchid, two are alike and placed horizontally. They are generally wider than the sepals. The third petal is different and is called the lip or labellum.

LIP: The lip is often the most spectacular part of the orchid flower. Brilliant color patterns may characterize this segment. It is usually larger than the other segments, but it may be smaller. It may be fluted or fringed.

There are numerous variations. On a slipper orchid the lip is the slipper or pouch. On a dancing lady the lip is the ballet skirt. On a vanda or phalaenopsis the lip is smaller than the other petals but is different in color and shape.

The lip is ingenious in design. Remember that the purpose of a flower is to attract a pollinator to pick up pollen, transport it and deposit it on another flower. Orchid pollinators may be bees, flies, birds, butterflies or moths. The lip may provide a landing spot for a flying insect. Bright colors, ridges and odors are guidance mechanisms that lead the pollinator to the nectar, and in the process it receives and deposits pollen.

Pollination is more complicated in some orchids. In some genera the visiting bee falls into the water in the bucket-shaped lip. In others the hostile male pollinator butts the flower with its head as though it is an enemy. Some orchids use fragrance to attract pollinators, which may imitate the smell of food or the female of the species.

COLUMN: The column contains the reproductive organs. On most flowers the stamens and pistils are separate parts, but in orchids they are fused into one part. Orchid flowers are bisexual, having both male and female parts, with a few exceptions where separate male and female flowers are produced.

The column appears in the center of the flower with the sepals and petals surrounding it, and is at the apex of all six parts. In many orchids the side lobes of the lip fold over the top of the column forming a tube, which along with the portion of the lip leading to it is called the throat.

The column is a complex structure that both disburses and receives pollen. In most orchids it is designed so the flower cannot pollinate itself. It is generally white and waxy. In a large cattleya type the column is about as big around as a pencil and an inch long. In a slipper orchid it is round and flat and called a staminode.

PEDICEL AND STEM: The ovary of an orchid flower is located behind the flower in a short stem called the pedicel. This stem may be attached to a multi-flowered inflorescence or directly to the plant. When a flower is pollinated, the sepals and petals wilt in due time and the pedicel which contains the ovary swells to become the seed pod.

NECTARY: Nectar is an attractant for the pollinating insects. It may be found, as in cattleya types, in a tube beneath the column extending down into the ovary. Other orchids, notably angraecoids, have visible spurs behind the flowers. Placement is designed to bring the visiting pollinator into contact with the reproductive parts so the flower can produce seeds.

Flower Production

The time of flowering depends upon one or more factors: inheritance, temperature, daylength, plant habit and growth habit.

For example, cymbidiums initiate their buds during the long days of summer so flower spikes develop during fall and winter and bloom in the spring. Night temperature affects the process, which makes it difficult

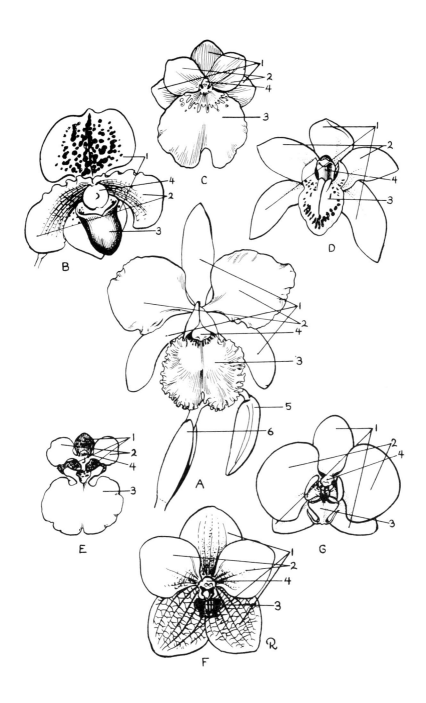

A. Cattleya; B. Paphiopedilum; C. Miltonia; D. Cymbidium; E. Oncidium; F. Vanda;
G. Phalaenopsis.
1. Sepals; 2. Petals; 3. Lip; 4. Column; 5. Bud; 6. Sheath.

to flower some cymbidiums in hot climates where there is not a temperature drop at night.

Phalaenopsis can be triggered into bloom by a drop in night temperatures, and normal spring flowers may be followed by secondary spikes if the nights are cool at that time.

Dendrobium nobile types need definite cooling plus a drying off period after growths are mature.

Daylength affects some orchids, just as it does chrysanthemums.

Hybrids in various genera or multigenera may be less demanding in their requirements and may bloom more easily and frequently than parent species.

Some orchids, such as cattleya types, bloom only once from a growth and not again until a new growth (pseudobulb) is matured. There are other orchids which bloom repeatedly from old growths along with the new. Evergreen dendrobiums are in this category.

Some terete vandas won't bloom if the sun is not bright enough or the days not long enough to suit them.

Cymbidium Oriental Legend

These three genera show the diversity in flower parts. (Top) Brassia bidens.
(Right) Renaglottis Clarence Russell, a hybrid. (Lower left) Angraecum leonis.

CATTLEYA ORCHID PLANT
(SYMPODIAL TYPE)

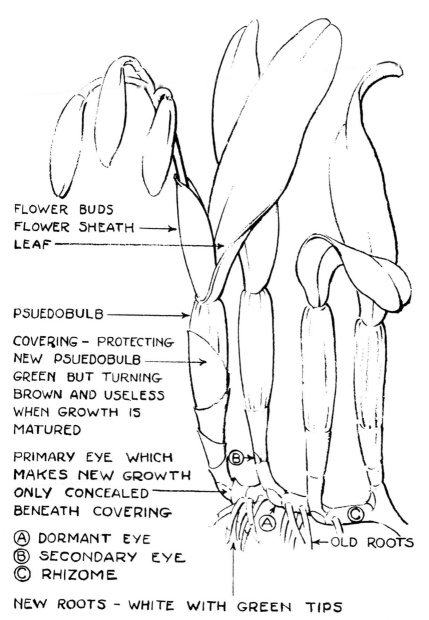

FLOWER BUDS
FLOWER SHEATH →
LEAF

PSUEDOBULB ——

COVERING - PROTECTING
NEW PSUEDOBULB ——
GREEN BUT TURNING
BROWN AND USELESS
WHEN GROWTH IS
MATURED

PRIMARY EYE WHICH
MAKES NEW GROWTH
ONLY CONCEALED
BENEATH COVERING

Ⓐ DORMANT EYE
Ⓑ SECONDARY EYE
Ⓒ RHIZOME

← OLD ROOTS

NEW ROOTS - WHITE WITH GREEN TIPS

BRUNO ALBERTS

CHAPTER II

THE PLANTS

You need to become acquainted with an orchid plant in order to grow it and bloom it. You need to understand its structure, behavior and habits.

An orchid plant is tough and strong, not fragile and delicate.

This is a plant that has struggled to survive in nature and has won out in competition with other tropical plants which may be gigantic in size by comparison. The orchid in the wilderness manages to get its share of sunlight, rain and air by taking to branches high up in the trees, growing on rocks in exposed places, often within reach of moisture from bodies of water or from fogs and low clouds in the mountains.

Some orchid plants look like succulents because of their thick leaves. Some are equipped to store up reserves of food and moisture to carry them through dry seasons in their habitats. These reserves help your plants survive if you neglect them, but cannot sustain them for very long.

You don't want to mistreat your orchids, nor should you kill them with kindness. So if you understand how the plants are put together, you will understand better how to keep them happy.

Basically the structure of an orchid plant is the same as any plant for it has roots, stems, leaves and flowers. But these parts are adapted to its way of life and differ somewhat from familiar plants which you grow in your garden.

Epiphytes and Terrestrials

Most of the cultivated orchids are epiphytes. They do not grow in the ground but instead grow in trees or on rocks. This puts their roots out into the air rather than underground. The word "epiphyte" means "air plant" or literally "to grow upon a plant." Pronounce it "EP-ih-fite."

Epiphytes are not parasites. They do not take anything from the host plant. Epiphytes perch upon other plants but get their moisture and nutrients from air, rain and debris. Mistletoe is a parasite whose roots penetrate the branches of host trees, sometimes killing them.

Cymbidiums and other orchids are terrestrials, which means "growing in the ground." Most of the native orchids of the United States, and all the natives of Europe are terrestrials.

Sympodial Orchid Plants

Two major types of growth are found in orchid plants.

One growth pattern is called sympodial. The other is monopodial.

For sympodial think of sideways.

An orchid with sympodial growth moves sideways. From a connecting stem which grows horizontally, it puts up successive growths in which each one is a duplicate of the one before.

Examine a cattleya type plant, or the sketch in this book. The upright growths are called pseudobulbs, each a repetition of the one before and growing parallel to each other. A plant may produce one new pseudobulb at a time, perhaps even only one per year. But it may make two or more new growths simultaneously, and a large plant may make several new growths at the same time. Hybrids may have more than one cycle of growth per year.

The majority of the cultivated orchids are sympodial — they grow sideways. New growth begins at the base of the previous mature growth.

Dendrobiums are sympodial, but make cane-type growths on some groups. Cymbidiums are sympodial with the connecting rhizome generally below the surface of the potting material. Paphiopedilums are sympodial but have no pseudobulbs.

Pronounce sympodial "sim-POH-dee-al."

There are five major parts of a sympodial orchid plant.

RHIZOME — The base of the plant is a hard, woody stem called a rhizome (rhymes with "home" and is pronounced "RHY-zohm"). It is the connecting or horizontal coupling between the pseudobulbs that grow upright. The rhizome creeps along on top or just below the surface of the potting medium. The rhizome is visible on plants growing on slabs. In a unifoliate cattleya the rhizome is about the thickness of a pencil and about an inch between bulbs. It starts out green but becomes brown. It is woody like a stem, which is what it is. On some orchids such as oncidiums or paphiopedilums the growths are so close together that the rhizomes are not visible. On some bulbophyllums the bulbs are spaced quite far apart and dangle from the rhizomes like keys on a chain.

PSEUDOBULB — The stem which rises from the rhizome and is the part of the plant between rhizome and leaf is called a pseudobulb, pronounced "SOO-doh-buhlb." "Pseudo" means "false" and this is not a true bulb although it functions like one in being a storage organ. The pseudobulb serves to store moisture and food which make it possible for an or-

SYMPODIAL TYPE ORCHID PLANTS

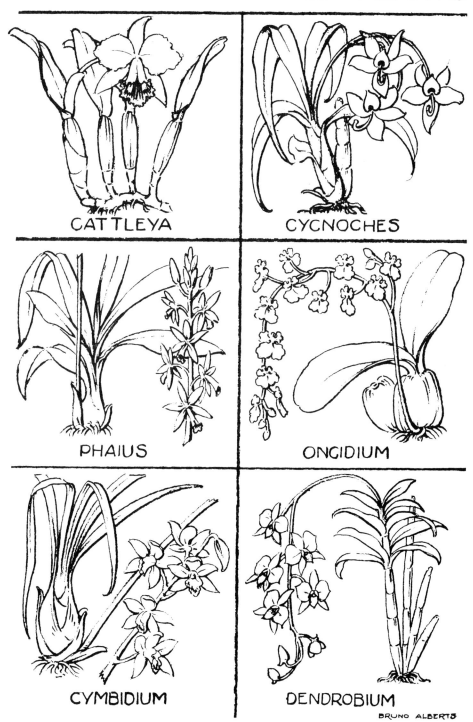

CATTLEYA

CYCNOCHES

PHAIUS

ONCIDIUM

CYMBIDIUM

DENDROBIUM

BRUNO ALBERTS

Compare these three sympodial plants. (Top) Bifrenaria harrisoniae blooms from the base of bulb. (Lower left) Dendrobium Golden Blossom produces flowers all along the canes. (Right) Encyclia cordigera blooms from top of egg-shaped bulbs with strap leaves.

chid plant to live in a climate where there is a dry season, as is the case in many parts of the tropics.

The size and shape of the pseudobulb varies with the genus and the species. See illustrations. Pseudobulbs may be a foot high — or more. They may be round and flat or tall and slender, egg-shaped, long and pointed like a cow's horn, or as small as nailheads on some miniatures. Cattleya guttata may have slender pseudobulbs four feet high and finger width. Some encyclias have pseudobulbs about the size and shape of hen eggs. Some oncidiums have bulbs like round green turtles.

Rarely does one bulb constitute a self-sufficient plant. The growing bulb draws on reserves of the previous bulbs for strength. On cattleya types it is desirable to have three or four pseudobulbs to support a new growth, but cymbidiums may be sold by the bulb. Catasetums, cycnoches and a few others can get along with one mature bulb to support the new growth.

LEAVES — Leaves come singly, in pairs, in series, or in multiple numbers. There is great variation in the sizes, shapes and textures of orchid leaves.

The function of a leaf is the process of photosynthesis, which makes the plant grow, as opposed to the function of a flower which is to attract a pollinator to make seed and produce the next generation.

Some orchids, like unifoliate cattleyas, have one leaf on top of the bulb. Cymbidiums have several pairs of long leaves which arch gracefully upward from the sides of the bulbs. Some orchids have terete leaves that are round like pencils, some have strap-like leaves, and others have broad veined foliage.

Most orchids are evergreen but shed their oldest leaves in due time as the plant grows and makes new leaves. The loss of back leaves on sympodial plants or lower leaves on monopodials is natural attrition as long as it happens gradually and the plants continue to make new growth.

Some orchids are deciduous and shed their leaves for a rest period, generally during cold or dry seasons.

The process of photosynthesis, which takes place in all green leaves, produces the oxygen we breathe as a by-product. The green coloring in the leaf, the chlorophyll, manufactures starch and sugar in the presence of light using nutrients, gases and water that have been absorbed by roots and leaves. The difference between the atmosphere of the earth and of the moon is that earth has green plants to conduct photosynthesis.

SHEATH — A cattleya type plant has a green sheath growing out of the top of the pseudobulb next to the leaf. It is about the size and shape of a knife blade. This is the protective covering for the buds while they are very small. It has two sides and the buds come up between them. Bulb, leaf and sheath all reach maturity at about the same time. A growth on a mature plant which does not make a sheath is called blind and probably

VANDA ORCHID PLANT
(MONOPODIAL TYPE)

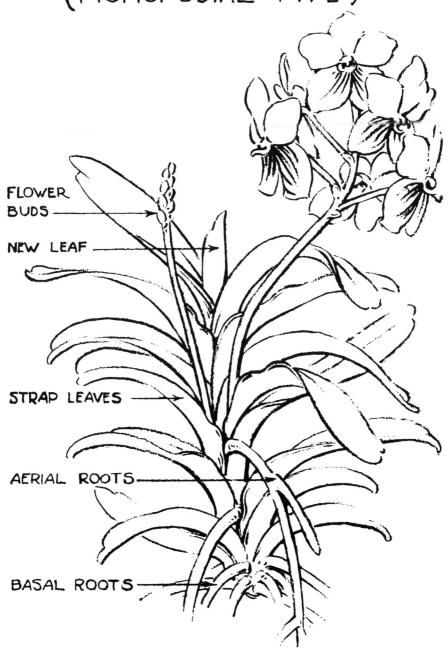

FLOWER
BUDS

NEW LEAF

STRAP LEAVES

AERIAL ROOTS

BASAL ROOTS

BRUNO ALBERTS

will not flower. Seedlings seldom make sheaths until they approach flowering size.

On some sympodial orchids the sheath may be smaller and almost hidden between the leaves. Some sympodial plants do not make sheaths. Some flower from the bases of the bulbs or along the stems.

ROOTS — The roots grow from the rhizome. They are white and fleshy with a spongy covering layer. The growing tips are bright green, reddish-brown or olive color. As with roots of all plants, the growing tip is pushed forward by the division of the cells immediately behind it.

Roots take up water and nutrients for the growth of the plant. On orchids they also serve as holdfasts, attaching themselves to the insides of containers, into the slabs of cork or tree fern, or even attaching to the plastic peanuts used for drainage material in pots. Roots often venture over the edges of pots or baskets, hanging out in the air as they do in nature.

When growing in the wild, roots may secure themselves in the cracks of bark and rocks. They absorb water and nutrients from the debris that collects around them.

Old roots on a plant may cease to function and turn brown and dry or brown and soggy. These may be cut off. However, as long as roots have a green core, they are useful, and experiments show that old live roots take up as much nourishment as do new roots.

HOW A SYMPODIAL PLANT GROWS — Sideways. A sympodial orchid plant makes successive growths and each complete growth (rhizome, pseudobulb, leaf, sheath, and flower) represents a complete cycle.

The growth pattern begins with an eye, the embryonic state of the next growth at the base of the newest pseudobulb. On a cattleya it appears as a triangular-shaped bump right where the bulb curves upward from the rhizome. Generally there are two eyes on opposite sides of the bulb, and a third or reserve eye slightly higher. One or both of the primary eyes may develop, the reserve is just that, a spare in case of disaster. Without a good green eye, a plant cannot grow and will die.

However, there may be undeveloped green eyes on older bulbs. If the oldest bulbs have visible good eyes, they may be cut off during repotting and grown into new plants. See Propagation chapter.

When the eye begins to grow horizontally, it soon turns upward and the horizontal section becomes the rhizome which becomes woody and brown. Growing parallel to the previous bulb, this new growth is called a lead until it becomes a mature bulb. The lead does not begin to plump up until it reaches full growth. It may be covered, as on cattleyas, with a green cover which later turns brown and papery. It may be peeled off when it becomes dry, but great care must be taken not to peel off the dormant eyes along with it.

MONOPODIAL TYPE ORCHID PLANTS

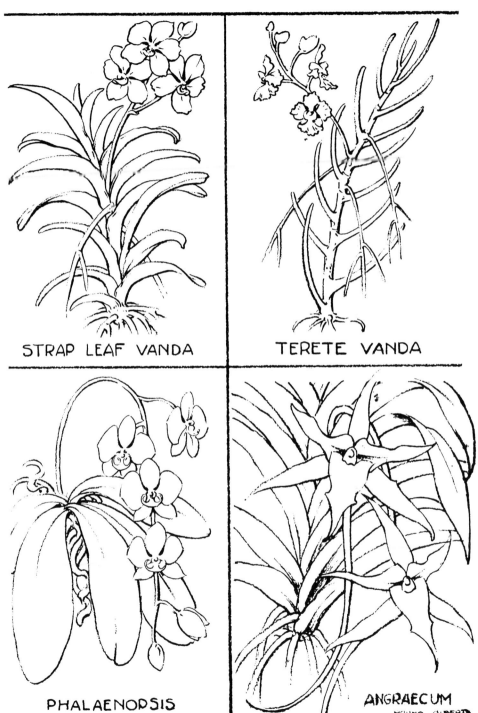

STRAP LEAF VANDA

TERETE VANDA

PHALAENOPSIS

ANGRAECUM

BRUNO ALBERTS

A new growth on a cymbidium appears as a sturdy, green roundish growth pointing upward at a slight angle from the base of the mature bulb. After it gets several inches high it begins to differentiate its leaves, and when mature the plump shape of the bulb can be seen.

A new growth on a paphiopedilum appears as a pair of little green leaves at the base of the last growth.

Monopodial Orchid Plants

Entirely different from the sideways growth of a sympodial orchid is that of a monopodial-type plant. Monopodial means "one foot." Pronounce it "mon-oh-POH-dee-al."

A monopodial orchid has neither pseudobulbs nor rhizomes. It grows continuously upward from the top of the plant. It produces roots and flowers at intervals from the vertical stem.

STEM — The single center support of a monopodial orchid may be a visible stem or a stem hidden by overlapping leaf bases.

Monopodial plants grow continuously taller, and some reach many feet in height under ideal conditions. Think of the terete vandas, arachnids and renantheras growing outdoors in the tropics. Others have reasonable height limits, such as the phalaenopsis group.

LEAVES — Quite in contrast to the foliage habit of a sympodial orchid, a monopodial orchid has alternate leaves the entire length of the stem. Lower leaves may fall off as the plant ages.

Leaves take quite different shapes and sizes. On strapleaf vandas they are like green bands arching horizontally from the vertical stems. On terete vandas the pencil slim stems and round blunt horizontal leaves look about alike. Angraecums generally have strap-like leaves. Phalaenopsis have broad leaves, glossy, thick and held horizontally.

ROOTS — Aerial roots are produced at intervals along the main stem and grow out and down. Some attach to the support, if it is a slab or a totem, some go down into the potting mix in a basket or pot, but many monopodial plant roots hang in the air. Many originate above the lower leaves. Active roots are white with green or brownish tips when in growth. Dry dead roots look like brown strings and may be cut off if their central core is brown.

FLOWERS — A monopodial orchid plant does not have flower sheaths, but it produces an inflorescence from the main stem just above a leaf. The inflorescence may be long, branched and multiflowered. Some plants produce several flower sprays at one time, some bloom continuously.

HOW A MONOPODIAL PLANT GROWS — Upwards. New growth comes out the top of the central stem.

A monopodial orchid has no pseudobulbs so it has no reserves of moisture and nutrients. Therefore, it never takes the decided rest that can be observed in sympodial types, but growth is slower during less optimum weather. The very nature of some monopodials, such as terete vandas with succulent round stems and leaves, equips them to withstand bright sun and daily drying by conserving moisture with a minimum of leaf surface exposed for evaporation.

Monopodial orchids have unseen eyes or growth points along their stems. These vegetative eyes generally remain dormant, but may be activated by something unusual. If the top of a vandaceous plant is broken off or damaged, or just bent, the stem may produce new growths (keikis) from eyes along the stem. Angraecums may grow into clumps by producing such multiple growths. Phalaenopsis that become leggy may be topped with the leaves and some new roots, and the leafless stump might put out new leaves and roots.

Ascocenda Rose Charm represents monopodial growth - upwards. Flower spikes come just above a leaf.

Doritaenopsis Mary McQuerry has fuchsia markings on yellow backgrounds.

Oncidium Kalihi is a curious yellow and brown flower. Single blooms come in succession at the top of stems three feet high · or more.

CHAPTER III

CULTURE

Orchids are different — not difficult.

Your plants will do their best to adapt themselves to the conditions you provide for them. But you must try your best to give them an environment that meets their needs. Before you buy a plant, ask yourself if your conditions are suitable for it.

Orchids do not need to be coddled. You can kill them with kindness.

The important thing is that you understand what your plants want, and give them the attention that helps them to reach their highest potential of growth and flowers.

Temperature, ventilation, light, water and fertilizer are the essential ingredients. The secret of success is a balance among these factors.

Temperature

Most cultivated orchids are happy in temperatures that are comfortable for people. If the air in your home or greenhouse feels good to you, it probably is suitable for your plants.

Some people think that because most of the epiphytic orchids come from the tropics they should be grown in hot, damp air.

Where orchids grow in the tropics it can get very cold at night, especially in the higher altitudes. Many orchid species grow within sight of high mountains in the Himalayas and the Andes, to say nothing of Mt. Kilimanjaro in Africa and Mount Kinabalu in Sabah (North Borneo). Darjeeling in northern India within sight of Mount Everest is home to over 600 species of orchids. The mists that drench the plants are icy, but this doesn't mean your orchids want to be very cold.

A difference between night and day temperatures is very important. Lower temperatures at night slow down the plants' respiration which in turn increases their growth. A general rule is to provide a drop of at least 10 °F if possible.

In the early days of orchid growing there were three greenhouses: the cool house, intermediate house and stove house. Now we know that many types of orchids can be grown together in a small greenhouse or on a windowsill.

Higher than normal temperatures need to be accompanied by higher humidity and moving air. Dry heat dehydrates plants, but warm moist air is desirable. If you live in a hot, dry climate, you need cooling equipment to lower the temperature and raise the humidity.

Ordinary garden plants begin to grow at about 40 °F, increase to an optimum at 84 °F, then slow down and cease to grow at 100 °F. Different plants have varying optimum ranges, and many orchids thrive between 75 °F and 95 °F. Growth may cease at lower or higher temperatures.

Most orchids do well if the minimum is about 55 °F. Most plants can endure lower temperatures for a short time, but flowers or buds may be damaged.

Temperatures too high can be as detrimental as those too low. Some plants find high temperatures very trying because the heat causes moisture to evaporate faster than the roots can take it up, causing plants to go into semi-dormancy in hot weather.

For example, vandaceous plants grow wonderfully well in Southeast Asia, but cattleyas do not perform as well there in the natural climate as in cooler climates with more variation between night and day. Cymbidiums are common garden plants in Southern California, but are more difficult to flower in North Florida where the night temperatures are too high in late summer for buds to initiate.

Many growers use cooling equipment in their greenhouses to temper heat and dryness. Home air conditioners take moisture out of the air. Wet pad coolers are better for greenhouses. If your greenhouse has heaters for winter and wet-pad coolers for summer, you can give your orchids nearly ideal conditions.

There are limits to the temperature compatibility of various genera. It would be difficult to try to grow masdevallias with the vandaceous, because the latter require more heat and light than cool-growing orchids can endure.

Ventilation

Most cultivated orchids are air plants. Ventilation is important. They must have fresh or circulating air, and they dislike stale, stuffy air. Air supplies carbon dioxide so necessary for plant growth. Photosynthesis combines water and carbon dioxide to make sugar in the leaf and disposes of the surplus oxygen into the air.

Ventilation is closely related to temperature.

Think of the breezes that blow around the orchids growing in the treetops. Give your indoor plants as much ventilation as possible, but

Two attractive hybrids in the Oncidium Alliance. (Top) Maclellanara Pagan Love Song has chartreuse-yellow flowers blotched with brown, many per spray. This is a trigeneric hybrid with three genera in its background. (Below) Miltassia Limbo Dancers has colorful flowers of yellow, brown and maroon. It is a bigeneric hybrid of Miltonia and Brassia.

avoid cold drafts and sudden changes.

Even on a chilly day you can open a top vent in the greenhouse, or crack a window in the plant room to make the air move. Hot air rises, so an escape opening up high moves the air at lower levels. A ceiling fan in the plant room improves the air circulation, and a turbulator running constantly in the greenhouse is great for the environment. A note of caution: suspend ceiling fans or turbulators above people's heads and preferably above the height of their raised hands, as an encounter with moving blades can be disastrous.

Moving air helps to prevent the spread of diseases by the reduction of standing water on flowers or foliage.

On warm days in humid climates, the greenhouse can be wide open and orchids will benefit from the fresh, moving air. If the temperature range and natural humidity are suitable, plants can be put outdoors in locations of compatible sunlight and shade. If growing conditions are appropriate, the orchids on a patio can be very decorative when in bloom.

In places like South Florida and the Caribbean where the trade winds blow, orchids outside may suffer from too much fresh air. Constant air movement may cause transpiration of moisture from leaves and bulbs faster than the roots can take it up. A windbreak will help, or a location that is sheltered from the prevailing breeze.

Orchids need air at their roots, too, and this is why the potting mix is porous — to permit air to enter and water to disperse rapidly. Orchids are grown in baskets, on slabs, or in a loose medium to meet this requirement. Greenhouses benches are best if made from an open material rather than having solid surfaces.

Light

Orchid plants need sunlight. Light is used to turn moisture and nutrients into plant growth. A good rule is to give your plants as much light as they can stand without scorching. While too much light may damage the plants, too little light will prevent flowering or cause weak growth.

For instance, cattleya plants that are a beautiful dark green color are handsome but may not flower, as they probably are not receiving enough light. The most productive cattleya type plants are a light green bordering on yellowish-green.

Remember that in nature most orchids grow high in the treetops, and if the trees are deciduous the orchids may be exposed to full sun at certain seasons. Bear in mind, too, that up high the air is moving constantly, there is moisture in mist and dew, so the hot sun is not a dry sun.

A spring flowering hybrid, Laeliocattleya Irene Finney, has pink-lavender flowers with deep rose lips and yellow throats.

Many of the slipper orchids grow in the ground beneath the trees, but even so must have adequate sunlight.

Too much sunlight is indicated by scorched spots on the foliage or pseudobulbs where the sun hits directly. The spot may be light at first, then turn darker like an iron scorch on a piece of cloth. Rarely does sunburn discolor an entire plant, only the portion of the green parts that is hit by direct sun for too long a period. Often a burned plant can survive, but if a strapleaf vanda, for instance, is burned all along the spine, it may lose so many leaves that it dies. If you change a plant's location, watch it carefully for a few days. Increased light should be given gradually and reactions noted.

Actually the burn damage is caused when the plant tissue gets too hot. If a leaf feels hot to your fingers, it may be burning. If you can cool down the leaf temperature with moving air and water, then the light can be brighter without doing any harm.

Morning sun is more beneficial to plants than afternoon sun, as morning is the active time for photosynthesis, the mysterious process by which plants form carbohydrates. Therefore, your greenhouse or growing area should be located to get maximum sun early in the day. A windowsill chosen for orchids should face east or south.

Growing orchids under artificial lights is possible and many hobbyists are doing this in apartments, high-rises, basements and family rooms. Cultural practices need to be geared to the light intensity and generally dry indoor conditions. Choose orchids that grow in low or medium daylight situations, avoiding those that need full sun. Size of plant is a factor, and while phalaenopsis and paphiopedilums are suitable, so are many other plants. The interest in indoor growing has stimulated interest in miniature types.

Watering and Humidity

There is a distinct difference between the terms "watering" and "humidity."

WATERING means providing moisture at the roots by pouring water into the container or onto the slab. Watering is one of the trickiest points of successful culture.

Most orchids do not want to be constantly wet at the roots. Rather, they want to be watered thoroughly and then allowed to dry out to some extent. Remember two rules. (1) If in doubt, don't water. (2) When you water, do it thoroughly. Never give just a little. A plant either needs water or it doesn't. Fill, the pot to the rim, let it drain, fill it again.

How often to water depends upon the temperature, the humidity, the kind and size of the pot, the type and density of the growing medium, the age and growth stage of the plant, and the plant's special requirements. The best way to manage all this is to group plants by genera or alliance in one place, with the sizes within this group together so you can water the small pots more often than the large ones. Separate plastic pots and clay pots as clay dries out faster.

You might water everything in your collection once a week; the phalaenopsis and paphiopedilums that have no pseudobulbs again at mid-week; and seedlings in small pots every other day. Plants on slabs get more air movement and the exposed roots need watering frequently.

(Opposite page) Center: Cattleya warscewiczii. Clockwise from top left: Schom-burgkia undulata; Encyclia cordigera; Oncidium lanceanum; Acacallis cyanea; Trichopilia suavis; Pescotorea lehmanni; Miltoniopsis vexillaria; Sobralia rosea; Phragmipedium longifolium.

Masdevallias like cool weather. This plant is perfectly at home in Bogota, Colombia.

Environmental conditions and watering schedules change with the seasons. Some plants, dendrobiums for instance, need frequent watering during warm weather but much less during their resting period in fall and winter.

In nature most orchids take a rest period during the dry season. Some must be forced to rest when grown in cultivation where environmental conditions are not as harsh as in the great outdoors. If not rested, they will make more vegetative growth instead of flowering.

Reducing watering during the rest period does not mean to dehydrate the plants to the point that the bulbs shrivel, nor does it mean to apply less water. Water thoroughly but less often.

One way to determine if a plant is in need of water is to poke your finger down into the potting mix and see if it is damp inside. Another way is to pick up the pot and feel how heavy it is. In time you will be able to determine if it feels heavy and wet or light and dry.

All of this is not as hard as it sounds. You will learn by experience and will be able to play it by instinct as your plants respond to your treatment.

Ascocenda Tiny Bubble in two shades of rose illustrates the checkered markings (called tessellations) found on many flowers in the vandaceous group.

Tap water as it comes from the hose is suitable in most places, but if your orchids are not thriving, have the water analyzed. Rain water is ideal, and orchids grown outdoors benefit from showers. Conversely, in places that have typhoons or hurricanes it may be necessary to move container plants to shelter in times of excessive rains.

In cold weather take care that water as it comes from the hose is not cold enough to shock the plants or damage the foliage. In the summer, run the hot water out of the hose before turning it on the plants.

A water breaker nozzle for your hose permits application of a great amount of water very quickly, which soaks the medium without washing it out of the pots or knocking over the small pots.

To water plants grown in the house, take them to the kitchen sink and run water through the pots thoroughly but gently. Let them drain in the sink for about an hour. Just pouring a little bit of water on top of the pot so it does not run out onto the table or plant stand does not water all the roots.

Too much water is worse than not enough. Watch your plants closely and you will learn to anticipate their needs.

Top to bottom: Doritaenopsis Corcata, Phalaenopsis Jack McQuerry, Dendrobium phalaenopsis hybrid.

Top to bottom: Cattleya guttata alba; Meristems of Laeliocattleya S.J. Bracey 'Wailani' AM/AOS and Brassolaeliocattleya Norman's Bay 'Low' FCC/RHS.

HUMIDITY — This refers to the moisture content of the air. Think about orchids in the wilds growing on rocks or trees near waterfalls, drenched by early morning mists or fogs, then dried off by the midday sun and brisk breezes.

You can raise the humidity in your greenhouse or growing area by putting moisture into the air. If you put a mist nozzle on your hose you can mist the plants, benches and walkways to raise the humidity. This also lowers leaf temperatures on hot days. Alternately, you can run water on the walkways and under the benches to raise the humidity in a few minutes with automatic or manual controls.

Do not mist your plants overhead on dull days or when the air feels damp and chilly. Don't mist late in the day when water won't evaporate from the foliage by nightfall. This invites diseases.

If you live where days are dull, such overhead misting may do harm. But if you have sunlight and moving air, the plants love it. If you live where nights are hot and there is not much temperature drop at sundown, misting foliage might be beneficial.

Raising the humidity to an acceptable level for orchids is the hardest part of growing them in your home. See Housing Chapter.

Fertilizer

Orchids in nature get extra nutrients from debris in crevices of tree bark or whatever surface their roots attach to. Orchids in cultivation benefit from addition of fertilizer to the growing medium.

All commercial fertilizers are labeled with three numbers. These show the proportions of available nitrogen (the first number), phosphorus (the second number) and potash (the third number). Minor or trace elements are usually included in a fertilizer mixture, including iron, copper, sulphur magnesium, and manganese.

Nitrogen, the first number, encourages growth. Phosphorous helps in production of flowers and then fruits. Potash aids in maturing growth and hardening plants off for a cooler or drier period of rest.

General recommendations are for a formula specified for orchids, at the rate of 10-10-10 or 18-18-18 or 20-20-20 for regular fertilizing. A higher ratio of phosphorous and potash, such as 10-30-20 encourages flowering and maturing of growth and should be given only when the growth cycle is completed. Orchids taking a definite rest period can go without fertilizer during that time unless they are growing in bark.

Plants grown in bark must have 30-10-10 fertilizer for the simple reason that the bark does not contain enough nitrogen for plant growth, and plants must have nitrogen to survive, Further, the wood-rotting fungus which breaks down the bark is voracious in its consumption of nitrogen and unless you supply it, the fungus will steal from the plant. If the fungus gets about 20% of the nitrogen, that leaves the plant with a balanced 10-10-10 fertilizer.

In climates where winter days are short and overcast, fertilizer must be reduced or withheld to compensate for lack of sunlight. When resumed, it should be done gradually with a diluted solution applied less frequently than during the height of the growing season.

Orchids without pseudobulbs, including paphiopedilums, phalaenopsis and the vandaceous group generally need fertilizer year round, although the frequency and dilution may be decreased in dull weather.

Cymbidium growers usually apply a balanced formula all year except during the growing season when a high nitrogen formula is used.

Follow the directions on the package for the dilution of the fertilizer in water. Do not think that twice as much is better. Half as much may be better but never double the strength or the roots may be burned.

It is important to apply fertilizer in enough water that it runs all through the pot. It is also most important to flush the pot with clear water between applications of fertilizer.

Plants can absorb nutrients through their foliage, so applying liquid fertilizer to the foliage as well as the roots is beneficial.

There are any number of gadgets that mix fertilizer and water. Just be sure to follow directions so the dilution is as prescribed.

There are granular slow-release fertilizers for orchids available. Again, it is important to follow directions so the application is effective but not overdone.

Correlation is the Key to Success

All of these factors of growth — light, air, temperature, moisture and fertilizer — are so closely related that your main effort must be to work out a balance.

Plants grown in bright light can use more water, fertilizer and moving air than plants grown in dim light. This is because sunlight is the energy which runs the chemical process which converts the various elements into plant food and then new growth. When the sun is bright, the process is more productive if the raw materials are there for the plant to work with.

On the other hand, plants in too much light shut down their manufacturing processes, as water which they need for the process evaporates too rapidly from the leaf surface. During periods of short days or overcast skies, the watering and fertilizing schedules need to be reduced to compensate for lower light.

Top to bottom: Vandachnis Premier, Vanda Rothschildiana, Ascocenda Yip Sum Wah.

Clockwise from top: Phaius tankervilliae; Paphiopedilum Edward Marshall Boehm; Paphiopedilum concolor; Ludisia discolor.

Temperature affects the rate of growth. A plant in a congenial range can function, whereas one that is too hot or too cold is not active and can't use the fertilizer and water as efficiently.

Water needs to be supplied in a ratio comparable to the rate the plant can use it, and sufficiently to offset moisture lost into the air. High humidity reduces moisture loss from the foliage, leaving more water within the plant tissues for use in the growth processes.

It all sounds very complicated but it really isn't. As you work with your plants you will sense any environmental factors that are out of balance.

When you get it all together and all the factors are in harmony, your plants will thrive.

Laelia anceps grows well on a cork slab. The roots adhere to the surface and penetrate the slab.

CHAPTER IV

POTTING

Potting of orchids is a controversial subject. Every grower has his favorite potting medium, choice of pot type, and ideas about when and how to repot.

There are people who are dedicated to tree fern, fir bark, charcoal, cork nuggets, sphagnum moss or rock. Some use mixtures and some constantly switch from one thing to another.

New media tempt people to make a switch, but if your plants are growing well and blooming, it is not wise to change everything for an unknown substance. Try a few plants if you wish, but give them a year or more to test their reactions before repotting an entire collection. What works in one environment may not do as well in another. Besides, you have to learn how to treat plants in a new medium.

If you are a beginner, leave your plants in the material in which they came, and get instructions for watering and fertilizing from the nurseryman from whom you bought these plants.

When and How to Repot

Most potting materials break down in time and need to be replaced before they become too dense and hold water to the exclusion of air.

Sympodial plants move forward, and walk right over the side of the pot, so repotting is necessary every year or two. Monopodial plants grow upward and may stay a long time in a basket or on a totem or a slab because most of the roots will hang out in the air.

A general rule is to repot a sympodial plant of the cattleya type when new roots and/or new growth are visible at the base of the youngest bulb. If you can do this when the new green and white root tips first appear in a little group, then the new roots can grow into the new medium. Sometimes the growth begins before the roots, which also signals time to repot. Seedlings may need repotting every six months because growth is fast and the medium may need changing in the small pots.

Choose a pot of a size that will accommodate two new bulbs, which generally means about one-third larger than the present pot unless you

Top to bottom: "Leopard orchid," Ansellia gigantea; Bulbophyllum vaginatum, Aeranthes grandiflora.

Cymbidium finlaysonianum (pendant); Cymbidium Mimi (miniature); Cymbidium Mauritius (standard).

are cutting off old back bulbs or dividing the plant. Do not be tempted to use a much larger pot because this wastes medium and bench space, and the medium will deteriorate before the plant fills the pot. If you have a specimen size sympodial plant that you don't want to divide, you might put it into a basket instead of a pot so the drainage is hastened and the medium in the center of the container dries out faster.

Remove the plant very carefully from the old pot. Most important, take care through the whole repotting process that you don't knock off the new eye or new growth at the base of the bulb that will become the new bulb.

If the potting medium is dry, it will be easier to get the plant out of the pot. Use a large flat kitchen knife to run around inside the rim to dislodge roots that are attached to the pot. Turn upside down and with one hand on the plant, tap the bottom of the pot. Watch that new growth!

With your fingers remove all the old potting mix from between the roots. Remember that old roots that are alive are valuable, but old dead roots from which the brown cover slips off, are useless. Cut dead roots off.

Examine the plant thoroughly, top and bottom. Remove any pests such as scale with a toothbrush. Cut off damaged leaves. Spray or dust cut surfaces with a fungicide, and spray the plant all over, especially the under-sides of the rhizomes, with insecticide.

Make a decision about dividing. If the plant has new bulbs and new growths in more than one direction, you need to choose. (See Propagation chapter.)

Put drainage material into the new clean pot first. Use crocks (broken clay pots), plastic "peanuts" used for shipping everything, pieces of charcoal, large pebbles, or what have you. If you use the plastic bits, put a rounded crock over the drainage hole lest one of these pieces clog up the hole.

Secure a stake to the side of the pot and have plastic wire or string ready. Place the back end of the plant against the side of the pot by the stake, hold it in place so that the rhizome is about an inch below the rim of the pot, fill around and under and between the roots, firming the medium with your thumbs or with a potting stick (like the handle of a small hammer) until the plant seems secure. Watch that green new growth! Don't knock it off.

Secure the plant in place with wire or string attached first to the stake and then looped around each bulb beginning with the one nearest the stake. Add a pot clip to hold down the rhizome. The rhizome must be on the surface of the medium. Don't bury it. Remove the pot clip when the roots take hold.

Return the label, tying it fast to a bulb or the stake. If label is brittle or the wording is faded, write a new label. A plant without a label is an orphan.

(Top) Dendrobium aggregatum hanging in a tree fern basket has flowers like showers of gold coins. (Right) This Angraecum eburneum grows in a 10-inch pot, its roots penetrate the 24-inch tree fern totem.

47

© 1972 Marion R. Sheehan

To repot a cymbidium, shake it out of the pot when a new growth appears. Shake off all old potting mix, cut off dead roots in the center and trim the good roots to about six inches. Check under and around the bulbs for pests such as sowbugs, millipeds, slugs and snails that like to hide in the crevices. Dust or spray cut surfaces with fungicide. Spray plant all over with insecticide.

Put crocks and premixed medium into the pot and under and around the roots so that the base of the new growth is almost level with the pot rim.

Paphiopedilums are small plants which grow compactly in small pots so it is not necessary to increase pot size every time you repot. But since the medium deteriorates, annual repotting is recommended.

New white tips on live roots help to distinguish which are viable and which are dead since all paphiopedilum roots are brown. Use your fingers to feel each root and if you can pull off the brown cover, leaving a brown thread, that root is dead and should be cut off. Leave live roots and don't trim them but examine them carefully for intruders.

Choose a pot as small as possible, put in ample crocks but don't block the drainage holes. Hold the plant in place in the center of the pot and work the medium up under the center, around the roots and out to the rim. The green parts should all be above the surface of the medium and about one inch below the pot rim. Stakes are not needed but pot clips may help secure the plants.

Plants growing in baskets present a problem in that some of their roots adhere to the slats but most roots hang outside. Mature plants can be left alone until the basket falls apart, with only the addition of some medium if the old material deteriorates or washes out. Young plants in small baskets can be set inside larger baskets, still in their small baskets, and medium placed around them.

If plants on slabs outgrow their supports or the support deteriorates, the best thing is to attach what remains of the old support to a new larger piece. This is best done at the beginning of the growing season. New roots will take hold.

Sanitation

Always use clean pots. Scrub used pots in water and detergent with a stiff brush and soak in a solution of one part Clorox to 10 parts water

(Opposite page) Clockwise from top left: Epidendrum ibaguense; Peristeria elata; Neomoorea wallisii; Masdevallia coccinea; Telipogon hemimelas; Anguloa brevilabris; Dracula wallisii; Anguloa clowesii.

Cymbidium Featherhill

for 30 minutes. Then rinse thoroughly and drain. Clean up your stakes, pot hangers, clips and drainage crocks at the same time lest they transmit disease.

Sterilize your tools before each use on a different plant. (See Problem chapter.)

Potting Media

With any potting medium that comes in a variety of sizes the choice depends on the size of the plant roots.

Plant on left needs repotting as roots of the new growth will be outside the pot. Plant on right has been repotted in tree fern, the old back bulbs removed. New lead faces center of pot with room to grow forward.

Mature vandas with roots as thick as pencils require a very open medium of chunky material so air is available. Phalaenopsis have roots of medium thickness and can use a medium grade of tree fern or bark, for example. Orchids with fine roots such as miltonias, and most seedlings do better in a finer medium. Their roots are small in circumference and can move easily through a fine medium, at the same time finding air pockets, yet they are able to snuggle comfortably into the material.

TREE FERN (HAPUU) — Tree fern fiber, harvested from the trunks of tree ferns in tropical countries makes good potting material for many orchids. It comes as shredded fiber in several grades, small chunks, slabs, totems, logs, pots, baskets and balls. It is easy to work with.

Roots will penetrate totems, slabs, pots and baskets. Totems may be used to support large plants such as angraecums growing in large clay pots or wooden baskets.

OSMUNDA — This is the root of the cinnamon fern and was used almost exclusively for potting orchids in the USA prior to World War II. Now it is difficult to find due to the advances of civilization and it is scarce

51

and expensive. Also it is difficult to work with as all the mud must be washed out before use, and it must be packed very firmly into the pots. It holds water and plants in osmunda may not need watering as often as plants in other media.

BARK — Bark used for orchids is from certain fir trees, redwoods and Scotch pines.

Bark comes in various sizes with the fine used for small plants, medium and coarse for larger plants in larger pots. Bark needs to be soaked in water for a few hours before using as it is difficult to get it wet. Hot water hastens this process.

Orchids in bark need to be fertilized with a high nitrogen fertilizer. (See section on Fertilizer.)

MIXES — There are as many potting mixes as there are growers using them. Formulas containing bark, peat, tree fern, wood fibers and sphagnum moss are popular. Perlite, turkey grit, decayed oak leaves, charcoal and other substances may be included. If you buy your plants from a nursery that uses a mix, and the plants grow well for you, then it would be best to use the same mix from the same source when they need repotting.

ROCK — Various types of rock are used for orchids. Rock has the advantage of not disintegrating. The culture of plants in rock or simply in charcoal is different from culture in other media and needs to be learned by experience.

SPHAGNUM MOSS — This finds favor with some growers, and it is found in many parts of the world. Whether used in a mix or alone or with charcoal, the culture is distinctive and must be mastered.

TERRESTRIAL ORCHIDS — Phaius, calanthes and other terrestrials require a potting mix that may include soil, compost, dehydrated dairy manure and other elements to make a rich garden loam.

Containers

Just like the choice of media, the choice of pot types depends on what works best for you. The controversy between the clay pot growers and the plastic pot growers is spirited. But the fact remains that what does best for your plants is what you should use.

CLAY POTS — Clay pots have been the standard containers for over a century. They come in many sizes. Some growers prefer those with slit sides, some like the shallow types for community pots and seedlings.

Clay pots are porous, permit evaporation through the sides as well as from the surface of the medium. Roots are a few degrees cooler in clay than in plastic containers.

PLASTIC POTS — Plastic pots are not porous, which cuts down the frequency of watering. They do not accumulate fertilizer salts on their surfaces. Small seedlings in square plastic pots grow well placed rim to rim as there is no air movement between the pots to dry them out.

BASKETS — Baskets for hanging plants should be made of durable, non-rotting wood or of plastic. It may be necessary to line the basket with fine wire or plastic screen to keep the medium in place.

Since baskets hang in moving air and are open, the media dry out more rapidly than in pots on a bench and watering needs to be more frequent. Many plants extend their roots out of the baskets into the air. Baskets are good for orchids that like bright light and can be hung up near the glass, for plants with pendant flower spikes like some aerides and rhynchostylis, and especially for stanhopeas that bloom from the bottom of the plants.

TUBS — Wooden boxes or tubs are fine containers for large cymbidiums. They should be constructed with the bottoms raised slightly above the base of the sides so drainage holes don't clog up.

SLABS AND LOGS — In nature, epiphytic orchids grow on tree limbs, in rock crevices and sometimes on decaying wood if their host tree fell to the ground. The advantage of using a slab or log of cork or treefern is that it is not necessary to repot except to attach it to a larger size in due time. Plants can be attached with plastic wire, hairpins or florist's staples. You can work a bit of sphagnum moss, redwood fiber or other substance around the roots if you wish to help keep them moist until plants attach themselves to the support. Rattail oncidiums such as Oncidium jonesianum which like to be kept relatively dry grow beautifully on hanging slabs.

Large slabs may be used for a colony of plants of one kind, either seedlings or keikis. Some of the miniature bulbophyllums and other genera that have long rhizomes between the bulbs and grow in several directions, do well on slabs. They can be trained by attaching with wire staples to make a solid mass.

UNCONVENTIONAL CONTAINERS — A driftwood tree or a strawberry jar planted with several identical plants makes an attractive decoration when in bloom. If you want to use blooming plants for indoor decoration, try planting a bifoliate cattleya on a horizontal cork slab and grow it in this position. then when it blooms, bring it indoors, set the slab on a silver tray, and you have an instant centerpiece.

DIVISIONS AND PROPAGATIONS

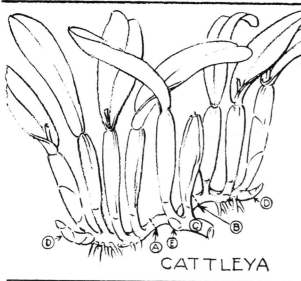

OLDER CATTLEYA PLANTS
ACCUMULATE MORE
PSUEDOBULBS AND LEAVES
REQUIRING DIVIDING
FOR REPOTTING

(A) CUT RHIZOME FOR
FOUR BULB DIVISION

(B) FOR THREE BULB
DIVISION

(C) LEAVING A TWO BACK-
BULB PROPAGATION

(D) NEW GROWTH ON
EACH DIVISION

(E) DORMANT EYE
ON BACK BULBS

CATTLEYA

(A) CUT FOR
TOP DIVISION

(B) KEIKI
(BABY PLANTS)

VANDA

(A) PLANTLETS
GROWING FROM NODES
CUT OFF AND
POT SEPARATELY —

DENDROBIUM

BRUNO ALBERTS

CHAPTER V

PROPAGATION

There are two ways to propagate (multiply) plants. By seed, which is the sexual method of placing pollen from one flower onto another, and growing plants from the seed in the pod that develops. The other way is by vegetative means, by which a new plant is produced from another plant and is an exact replica of it.

Vegetative Propagation

DIVISIONS — A mature sympodial plant that is making two new leads in different directions simultaneously and has three or four bulbs with leaves to support each lead may be divided into two separate plants. These may be expected to flower regularly without interruption.

The time to make divisions is at repotting time. When a plant shows a new lead (growth) forming, and tips of new roots, this is the time to divide. (See Chapter IV on Potting.)

When you get the plant out of the pot, remove all the old medium around the roots and then see how it grows. You may have enough new leads and supporting bulbs to make two or three divisions, and you may have some live back bulbs as well.

Check for old live roots on each piece that you propose to cut loose. Cut off brown leafless back bulbs and discard. Green back bulbs, beyond what are needed for support of a new growth, may be saved.

A consideration when making divisions is whether you want one large specimen plant that will have multiple blooms or two or more pots of the same plant. Do you have space for extra pots? Greenhouses fill up quickly.

Paphiopedilums tend to break into divisions when taken out of the pots, but stronger plants will develop if there are multiple growths rather than single growths. Two mature growths to each new one are desirable. Paphs make a good show if allowed to grow into large clumps.

Cymbidiums when divided should have three or more bulbs to support each new growth. The best flowerings are on large plants. However, when a plant has several leafless pseudobulbs in the center, dividing is overdue.

Two yellow and red orchids. Sophrolaeliocattleya Mary McQuerry has butter
yellow sepals and petals and a red lip. Phalaenopsis Solar Flare has red
markings on yellow sepals and petals.

BACK BULBS — When a sympodial plant has enough bulbs to support a new growth plus two or three inactive but still green bulbs at the back of the plant, the back bulbs may be induced to grow into a new plant.

If left alone, back bulbs give support to the front of the plant, but if severed, they may make an effort to stay alive.

Back bulbs may not have any live roots, but they must have at least one good green eye.

You can pot up back bulbs in small pots by securing them with pot clips and stakes so they don't wobble and break any emerging roots. Or you can put them into a container of damp sphagnum moss or seedling bark in a shady place. Kept damp they may begin new growths, which may then be potted up. Such back bulbs take a few years to make normal sized growths capable of supporting flowers.

Leafless cymbidium back bulbs may or may not make new growths when treated in this manner. A better type of cymbidium division is a single bulb with leaves with an attached back bulb.

TOP CUTTINGS — Some of the monopodial orchids, notably the vandaceous group, may be propagated by top cuttings, if you want two plants instead of one. Or if the one has become so tall it is unmanageable.

A top portion with at least six pairs of leaves plus a few active aerial roots is able to survive as a separate plant. Simply cut horizontally through the main stem and put it in a container or attach it to a slab and mist it frequently for a while.

Leave the bottom part alone. It should sprout from the side from a dormant eye, but will not be perfectly symmetrical as it was before. Even leafless bases of vandas, if they have good roots, may put out new growth.

OFFSETS AND STEM PROPAGATIONS — Offsets are little plants that grow off some part of a mature plant, generally without help from the grower. Hawaiians call these "keikis," a word for baby.

Offsets may be removed from the parents when they begin to make their own roots.

Dendrobiums frequently produce keikis from the nodes along the canes. These may be sliced from the cane and potted separately. Better yet, make a colony of several cultivars in a pot or on a slab.

Phalaenopsis, especially of the Phal. lueddemanniana group, make offsets on the long flower stems, which may be cut off when they make roots, or curled back and anchored with staple-type clips on the potting surface or slab. Some phalaenopsis hybrids are induced to make plants from nodes on the flowering stems by use of a keiki-inducing substance.

Some vandaceous plants make keikis, especially if the main stem is bent. These may be left in place for a group effect, or removed and potted separately when they have their own roots.

Orchids from Seeds

Some people shy away from growing orchids because they think they will have to wait seven years for their first blooms. While this may be the case with orchids grown from seeds, this is not the correct approach for amateur growers. Orchids from seeds do take a long time and the process is tedious.

But you don't grow roses from seeds, do you?

The answer for hobbyists is to buy flowering size plants in bud or in bloom. When beginners get more experienced they can buy smaller seedlings at more reasonable prices. But seeds, no way.

The problem with growing from seeds is the selection of parents. The world is full of people with fine hybrids or varieties that are producing seed from selfings or hybrids. To cross two orchids just because they are in bloom at the same time is hardly worth the trouble. Read the sequence that follows and see if it is worthwhile for what might be mediocre results, and many plants of the same thing.

SEED — Two orchids are carefully selected as parents, chosen for specific qualities of the flowers. Hand pollination results, if successful, in the formation of a seed pod.

FLASKS — When the pod is mature (which may take several months) or still green (for embryo culture), the tiny dustlike seeds are planted in a solution of nutrients inside a sterile glass bottle under the most antiseptic conditions. Orchid seeds are without their own food supply. Beans, for instance, feed their sprouts from the fleshy part of the beans until roots and leaves can function. Orchid seeds are planted into special agar mixtures and sealed inside the bottles.

Eventually, if all goes well, green fuzz appears on top of the agar (planting medium) in the flask. Flasks may be transplanted once or more under sterile conditions.

COMMUNITY POTS — When the tiny plants are big enough to come out of their bottle incubators, several seedlings are planted into each pot in a potting mixture of fine texture. Their care is very important at this stage, like the care of babies.

SEEDLINGS — As seedlings, the little plants gradually move from the community pots through various pot sizes until they reach maturity. There may be many fatalities along the way.

Plants can be bought at any of these stages, from flasks on up, but the question to ask yourself is if you can properly care for them, and are you patient enough to wait for them to grow to maturity before they bloom?

Mericlones

There are many plants available called meristems or mericlones. They are vegetative divisions from one mature plant, and as such carry the varietal name and award, if any, of the mother plant. If well grown, they are identical to the mother plant, but mericlones in poor health will not show the full potential even though they are exact reproductions.

To make mericlones, a tiny piece of tissue is extracted from a growing point in the mother plant. It is put into a sterile bottle with agar, and continually cut into small pieces as it grows. The proliferations may be made indefinitely, but when cutting stops, the tiny pieces begin to develop into plants. Not all genera of orchids can be cloned with success.

Mericlones then are grown on just as are seedlings, through the small pots up to mature size. Mericlones cost less than mother plants or divisions of mother plants, yet should be identical when mature.

Mericlones are a good way to acquire fine cultivars or varieties at a reasonable price, but they do not replace the excitement of seeing seedlings bloom for the first time, nor are they as up to date as new seedlings since mericlones are already at least one generation old.

Some phalaenopsis make new plants called "offsets" or "keikis" on the old flower stems. These may be cut off and grown separately when roots appear on keiki.

Three interesting species. (Top) Laelia briegeri grows on rocks in full sun, has bright yellow two-inch flowers. (Right) Cirrhopetalum medusae has curious fragrant cream flowers on a dwarf plant. The lateral sepals are the long segments. (Left) Dendrobium loddigesii flowers at the nodes. Blooms are lilac with orange and white lips.

CHAPTER VI

ORCHID NAMES

Orchid names are easy when you get accustomed to them. Some of your people friends have strange names which become familiar in time. Orchid names will become easy as your plants become old friends.

FAMILY — The plant family name is Orchidaceae, pronounced "or-kih-DAY-see-ee." The family includes all the orchids. You may not like using this name in conversation, and reference to "the orchid family" is acceptable.

GENUS — Within the family are many genera. Genera is plural for genus. Genera is pronounced "JEN-er-ruh" and genus is "JEE-nus."

In an orchid plant's name, the genus comes first. Cattleya is a genus. So are Oncidium, Dendrobium, Cymbidium, Masdevallia and many more. The genus name may be abbreviated once it is established which genus is under discussion. The genus name begins with a capital letter.

So when you refer to Cattleya trianaei, the genus name is Cattleya and comes first. The species name is trianaei. Every genus is made up of many species. There are probably 30,000 species of orchids classified into about 600 genera. Species is pronounced "SPEE-sheez." The word species is both singular and plural. There is no such thing in horticulture as a specie — it is a species.

SPECIES — Species are plants originated in nature even though some plants are now in cultivation. Species names are in Latinized form. Cattleya mossiae was named for a Mrs. Moss. Species names begin with lower case letters.

HYBRIDS — Hybrids may be made by nature when two different orchid species are cross-pollinated by an insect or whatever, and these are called natural hybrids. Most orchid hybrids have been made by man . . . thousands of hybrids and more being made every day. A hybrid name looks like a species name in that the genus comes first and the hybrid name comes next. A hybrid with Cattleya warscewiczii and Cattleya mossiae as parents is named Cattleya Enid. The species names (mossiae and warscewiczii) are written with small first letters. The hybrid name and the genus name begin with capitals. The formula is written with a multiplication sign to indicate a hybrid: Cattleya Enid (C. warscewiczii × C. mossiae).

The hybrid name, Enid, is technically a grex epithet. Grex means a herd or a flock, and is the assemblage of all plants with the same hybrid name. Grex or hybrid names are in modern language, hence Enid. The registered hybrid or grex name applies to every plant produced by using these same two parents, whether or not they are the actual plants used the first time. Everytime a Cattleya warscewiczii and a Cattleya mossiae are crossed, the progeny are automatically Cattleya Enid.

Crossing two cattleyas is only the beginning because orchids of one genus will hybridize with orchids of some other genus. This makes a bigeneric hybrid, meaning two genera. Say it "bye-gen-EHR-ik."

Birds mate only with their own kind. You never see a bluejay with a red head because one parent was a woodpecker. Dogs, however, mix types so well that some are of unidentifiable ancestry. Orchids are like dogs. Mate a cocker spaniel with a dachshund and you have a mixed breed. Hybridize a Laelia and a Cattleya and you have a bigeneric hybrid, a Laeliocattleya.

Bigeneric hybrids in orchids are the first step, as there are multigeneric orchids with several genera in their ancestry. And whereas this type of mixed breed is not desirable in dogs, it makes show winners in orchids.

It is the ability of orchids to hybridize across generic lines that is producing fascinating flowers. New generic names are constantly being registered, as combinations are made for the first time or carried one step further. Five genera — six — seven — combined through generations into a new hybrid genus — the possibilities are endless.

You need not try to learn all the genera names. Just learn them as you become acquainted with plants carrying these names.

The originator who produces and flowers a new hybrid may name it and register the grex name with The Royal Horticultural Society in London which is the International Authority for the Registration of Orchid Hybrids.

VARIETY — A species plant may have a varietal name, which indicates a botanical variety found in nature. For instance, Cattleya skinneri normally has lavender flowers but some plants have white flowers. These are designated as Cattleya skinneri var. alba. The word "variety" is abbreviated and the varietal name begins with a small letter and is in Latin form, that is, "alba" instead of "white." Calanthe vestita is milky white, but Calanthe vestita var. regnieri has a rose-colored lip with a crimson blotch.

CULTIVAR — A species or a hybrid may carry a cultivar epithet (name)

Cattleya skinneri var. alba has white flowers, sometimes with lavender throats, produced in clusters. The lavender-flowered form of this Central American bifoliate species is more common than the white variety.

as well. A cultivar is a cultivated variety, with a name used to designate an individual plant and all of its vegetative propagations made by division or by mericloning. Example: Cattleya skinneri var. alba 'McQuerry' adds a cultivar name following in order, genus, species and variety. The cultivar epithet is in modern language, one to three words, begins with a capital letter and is enclosed in single quote marks.

If you have three different plants of Cattleya trianaei, you might name one 'Tom,' another 'Dick,' and another 'Harry.' But if you divide 'Tom' into two plants, both are still 'Tom' and you might need to add A-B-C to distinguish divisions or #1-#2-#3. People are inclined to speak of cultivars as varieties.

Mericlones, plants that are produced by meristem techniques from a piece of tissue from a mother plant, are vegetative reproductions and carry the cultivar name of the mother plant. Several cultivars of Blc. Norman's Bay have been cloned, so the cultivar name indicates whether it is Blc. Norman's Bay 'Low' or Blc. Norman's Bay 'Lucile.'

AWARDS — Plants that win awards must carry cultivar names to identify the particular clones.

About awards. Various orchid organizations give awards to outstanding plants. Thus Paphiopedilum Maudiae 'Magnificum' FCC/RHS indicates that this plant received a First Class Certificate from the Royal Horticultural Society (given in 1901). There are many divisions of this awarded clone in cultivation today. Many other clones of Paphiopedilum Maudiae have received various awards over the years, and each division of each awarded plant still carries the award designation. Mericlones are vegetative divisions which continue to carry awards, but seedlings are not and do not continue the award designation.

Other award designations include AM for Award of Merit, HCC for High Class Certificate, plus various other awards. Society initials include AOS for the American Orchid Society, AOC for the Australian Orchid Council, and many other regional and national organizations.

To recap: Cattleya (genus) skinneri (species) var. alba (variety) 'McQuerry' (cultivar).

Paphiopedilum (genus) Maudiae (hybrid or grex) 'Magnificum' (cultivar) FCC/RHS (award).

Colombian miltonias are displayed beautifully on a balcony and in a home during the 7th World Orchid Conference in Medellin.

BRASSAVOLA GLAUCA

Phalaenopsis with heavy red and mahogany spotting and "leopard lips" add interest to a collection. This is a French hybrid, Phal. Elise de Valec.

CHAPTER VII

THE ORCHIDS

Which orchids should you grow?

Will you be a specialist, growing only cymbidiums or cattleyas or vandas, depending on your geographic location? Will you concentrate on the slipper orchids or perhaps a mix of miniatures that take minimum space?

Will you be a collector of several types? Most small collections are mixtures, which makes for variety in flower types, sizes and color, blooming seasons and cultural practices.

Many different types of orchids will grow well together in the same environment providing they are reasonably congenial in their needs. You must choose according to the factors you can provide, especially minimum and maximum temperatures and light intensity.

The orchid nurseries publish fascinating advertisements and catalogs full of gorgeous color photos to tempt you.

Don't begin with expensive awarded plants, cheap imports or small seedlings. You must learn to grow orchids, so for your first ones choose blooming plants in pots that look healthy and sturdy. Beware of sickly or rootless plants that are bargains. Buy healthy, vigorous plants from reputable sources. We all kill a few plants along the way, but your chances are better in the beginning if your plants are healthy, mature and established.

Shop around. Visit the nurseries near home and in your travels. Write for catalogs. Study the ads. Visit other hobby growers. Go to orchid shows. Ask questions. Attend orchid society meetings. Enjoy!

Cattleya Alliance

Cattleyas are the most familiar orchids which come to mind at the mention of the word "orchid." There are over 60 species in this genus, some with large flowers and some with small blooms. Cattleyas are native to Central and South America.

Along with close relatives in other genera, this group has been hybridized into many bigeneric and multigeneric hybrids.

Cattleya Alliance plants and flowers come in many sizes. (Top) C. luteola has miniature yellow blooms on dwarf plants. C. Portia produces mid-size blooms in clusters on very tall bifoliate plants. (Opposite page) Potinara Ernest Walters has four-inch cerise flowers on plants of intermediate size.

CATTLEYA — Abbreviation C. Pronunciation "KAT-lee-uh."

There are two major groups. The unifoliate cattleyas have single leaves at the top of the pseudobulbs, bear large, showy flowers, and are the ancestors of today's large hybrids.

The bifoliate cattleyas have two or three leaves, generally placed horizontally, at the top of slender pseudobulbs. The bifoliates have smaller flowers than the unifoliates in a wide range of colors, some with spots, often with heavy substance, and frequently produced in clusters.

LAELIA — Abbreviation L. Pronunciation "LAY-lee-uh."

Laelias are smaller plants, generally, than cattleyas. There is considerable variation within the genus as to plant appearance and size, flower size and color, and growing habitats. Some laelias grow naturally on rocks and are designated as lithophytic or rupiculous (both meaning "to grow on rocks"), but most of them grow on trees primarily in Central America and Brazil.

While the flowers are often brightly colored and are grown for their own charm, the great value of this genus lies in its use in hybridizing to give color to the offspring. Laeliocattleya is a bigeneric combination of Laelia x Cattleya in which there are hundreds of hybrids.

BRASSAVOLA — Abbreviation B. Pronunciation "bra-SAH-voh-luh."

Brassavola digbyana is widely used in breeding to impart fringe to the lip of Cattleya hybrids. B. nodosa and B. glauca are used in hybridizing for other qualities. They are attractive plants on their own merits.

SOPHRONITIS — Abbreviation Soph. Pronunciation "sof-roh-NYE-tiss."

This is a small genus found only in southeastern Brazil and Paraguay. The plants are very small, as are the flowers but the vivid scarlet red color of Soph. coccinea has made it a favorite for hybridizing with larger flowers in the alliance.

HYBRIDS — Familiar names combining these genera include Brassocattleya (Bc.), Brassolaeliocattleya (Blc.), Laeliocattleya (Lc.), Sophrocattleya (Sc.), and Sophrolaeliocattleya (Slc.). Put the four genera above together and the name is Potinara (Pot.).

The use of other affiliated genera including Epidendrum, Encyclia, Schomburgkia, Diacrium, Broughtonia in assorted combinations makes interesting flowers.

CULTURE — The Cattleya Alliance plants are easy to grow. The temperature range that is comfortable for you is fine for them, that is, about 55°F minimum and about 85°F maximum. They need bright but not direct sunlight, moving air, adequate water and some fertilizer.

All plants of this group grow during the warm months of summer. Some make sheaths and bloom immediately, others mature their pseudobulbs and wait until spring to produce flowers. Noticeable resting periods for the species should be observed with less frequent watering and less fertilizer.

Seedlings need slightly less light but may need watering more frequently because their small pots dry out rapidly.

A display of multicolored reed-stem epidendrums at a flower show.

Epidendrum/Encyclia

Abbreviation Epi./Enc. Pronunciation "ep-ih-DEN-drum/"en-SICK-lee-uh."

In the Cattleya Alliance, Epidendrum comprises a vast genus found in tropical and sub-tropical America, with Epi. conopseum growing as far north as the east coast of North Carolina. There may be a thousand species.

Because of their size and diversity, it is impossible to give cultural directions that fit them all, but the guidelines under Cattleya Alliance are a start. Most are easy to grow and floriferous.

The reed-stem epidendrums grown in tropical gardens are colorful and sunloving, have rounded heads of bright starry flowers on tall slender stems.

Many species formerly classed as Epidendrum have now been labeled Encyclia, including the bulbous types. Many have showy flowers. They are readily hybridized with others of the Cattleya Alliance, but still registered as Epidendrum in hybrid lists.

Familiar species are Encyclia cochleata, the "cockle-shell" orchid; Encyclia cordigera, with fuchsia lips and curling chocolate sepals and petals, formerly known as Epidendrum atropurpureum, and Encyclia mariae, used in hybridizing for its green petal color.

Cattleya granulosa has olive-green flowers spotted with maroon. The white lip is veined crimson. Flowers are heavy and waxy. This bifoliate species is native to Brazil.

J.Nugent Fitch. del. et lith.

R.S.Williams & Son. Publrs.

EPIDENDRUM AMABILE

Cymbidium

Abbreviation Cym. Pronunciation: "sym-BID-ee-um"

A greenhouse full of cymbidium blooms is dazzling. There are many colors, mostly pastels. The greens and yellows are vivid, the pinks are lovely and the odd shades fascinating.

The number of flowers and the durability of the blooms adds to the value of these orchids.

Cymbidiums have been developed to a high degree of perfection. The finest flowers are round, clear and sparkling. New hybrids are coming on the market all the time. By studying awarded plants at shows and in greenhouses, you can observe the features that make high quality flowers.

Unlike cattleyas, cymbidiums have been hybridized with only three other genera to date, the hybrids being novelties rather than major genera. The cymbidiums in cultivation have been developed through many generations from a few species.

The majority come into bloom in the spring, providing florist flowers for Easter and Mother's Day. Sprays may last a month when cut, and individual blooms on the plants may last much longer. Flowers should be open for about ten days before being cut.

Cymbidium flowers are on the market year round because flowers from the Southern Hemisphere are sent north when it is spring down there. Flowers from Australia and South Africa supply markets in the United States and Europe during the off season.

Cymbidiums come from India, southern China, down the eastern part of Australia and the countries in between. Today's fine hybrids are mostly derived from species that are native to the Himalayan regions of Asia where the nights are cool.

Miniature cymbidiums are popular with hobby growers because they take less space than standards. The flowers are easier to bloom in warmer climates, as they are developed using standard forms with small species from Japan, China and Australia.

POTTING MIXTURES — Every grower has his choice of containers and media. Some grow cymbidiums in garden beds where the climate is suitable. The best route if you are a beginner with a few cymbidiums in pots is to buy the potting mix at the nursery the plants came from. Whatever the mixture, it should have a base of good compost or humus plus ingredients that will speed the drainage such as gravel, small bark, coarse sand, peat, redwood fiber or perlite. It should be high in organic matter and have a pH of about 6.0. (See Chapters on Potting and Propagation.)

The lip on this chalk white Cymbidium Pearl-Balkis is stippled with burgundy. Cymbidiums grown for cut flowers are shipped all over the world and are available all year. (Below) A nursery in South Africa.

CULTURE — Cymbidiums should never be dried out, but more water is needed in summer than during the cool season when the plants are resting.

Overhead mist spraying benefits plants on hot, bright days to raise the humidity and reduce the evaporation. Water should be of neutral or slightly acid pH.

Fertilizer formulas specified for cymbidiums may be applied all year long, with extra nitrogen added during the growing season.

Bright light is important. Cymbidiums growing in the ground do best under spreading trees where the light and shade patterns are constantly moving. Air movement is most important to good growth.

Temperature seems to be a critical factor in inducing cymbidiums to set buds because they need a drop in night temperature in late summer and early fall. In hot climates this can be helped by cooling equipment.

During growth temperature can go up to 90 °F providing there is moving air and overhead mist to protect from bright sun. The factors must be correlated. A daytime range of 75 °F to 80 °F is better. A night temperature of 50 °F is desirable, but this is not always possible in a hobby collection. Nights should be considerably cooler than days at the time of bud initiation by 20 to 30 degrees.

In winter, plants can stand very cool temperatures, some endure light frost, but night temperatures higher than 60 °F may cause buds to drop.

Seedlings can be grown with higher night temperatures all year to encourage growth. Less light intensity and higher humidity than given mature plants are recommended for seedlings.

Phalaenopsis

Abbreviation Phal. Pronunciation: "fal-en-OPP-siss"

Phalaenopsis are easy to grow where there is sufficient warmth. Because they can grow in subdued light, they are amenable houseplants. Because they are medium or small size plants, they take less space than many other orchids and are suitable for windowsill or artificial light growing arrangements. The reward in flowers is great, as many of them produce long sprays of durable blooms that may last for more than a month singly, or over a few months for a long spray. By growing phalaenopsis hybrids and doritaenopsis hybrids you can have flowers almost all year.

White phalaenopsis are brides' orchids, being unsurpassed for wedding flowers. But there are intriguing phalaenopsis flowers in a vivid array of colors with new ones coming along every day.

Large and small pinks make showers of flowers and some of the doritaenopsis hybrids produce dark pink, fuchsia, and magenta blooms.

Phalaenopsis stuartiana is a Philippine species, white spotted with cinnamon, that is used in breeding spotted hybrids.

White flowers with red lips are attractive. Small flowered types bred from Phalaenopsis lueddemanniana have interesting colors with blooms in succession over long periods.

Yellow phalaenopsis have been combined with other colors for sunset shades, some with colored lips, spots or stripes.

Novelty phalaenopsis are those using some lesser known species to produce flowers of bronze, chartreuse and other off shades. Flowers with spots, stripes and "leopard lips" are fascinating.

CULTURE — Phalaenopsis come from warm areas of Southeast Asia and the plants need to be warm all year. They grow best in a range between 65 °F and 85 °F providing there is sufficient humidity at the higher figures. A drop to 55 °F at night for three or four weeks initiates flower spikes.

Phalaenopsis generally flower in late winter and spring, having set their buds and started their spikes in the fall. On the West Coast of the USA where the nights are cool all year, phalaenopsis set more second, third and even fourth spikes than here in the Southeast where the summer nights are warmer.

Spotted phalaenopsis vary in size, shape and color. (From top)
Phalaenopsis Diane Hartman; Phalaenopsis Mambo; Phalaenopsis
Golden Grant.

Phalaenopsis Princess Kaiulani is a primary hybrid, a cross of Phal. violacea x Phal. amboinensis.

Many phalaenopsis can be persuaded to make secondary spikes after flowers are cut if a few nodes on the old inflorescences remain and conditions are suitable.

Phalaenopsis like to be constantly moist, and it is important that the medium drains quickly because watering should be frequent. Water should be warmed in winter if it is cooler than the air temperature. Watering should be done early in the day so the foliage is dry by night. Crown rot is generally caused by water standing in the crown (between the top two leaves) during low temperatures.

Phalaenopsis are monopodial plants and have no bulbs but they have succulent leaves and vigorous roots. Any fertilizer used for other orchids is suitable, but if potted in bark a 3-1-1 formula is necessary. A high nitrogen like 20-10-10 during the summer with any other media may stimulate growth. Feeding can be frequent during warm weather and active growth, but the dosage should be at or below the product recommendation. Clear water should be given between every few applications of fertilizer to wash out the salts.

Phalaenopsis can do with less light than many other orchids because their big leaves burn easily. A range between 1,000 and 1,800 foot candles is suitable. However, if you provide humidity and moving air, light can be brighter with proper water and fertilizer, growth will be more vigorous.

Seedlings should be grown in more shade. Recently potted plants should be shaded until growth resumes.

**Phalaenopsis Teoh Phaik Khuan has large
pink flowers striped with darker pink.**

Air movement is essential to good health of phalaenopsis, but it must
be warm and moist. Cold drafts and sudden changes harm plants and cause
buds to drop. Air movement is needed when flowers are open to prevent
spotting of the blooms by botrytis.

Doritis/Doritaenopsis

Abbreviations Dor./Dtps. Pronunciation "dor-EYE-tiss"/"dor-eye-ten-
OPP-siss."

Phalaenopsis crosses with Doritis pulcherrima in the background make
hybrids with the best of both parents, getting from the small Doritis the
tendency to bloom in summer, and extension of the color range, and
somewhat heavier substance. Size of the hybrids has reached that of
straight Phalaenopsis.

MULTIGENERIC HYBRIDS — Phalaenopsis have been crossed with
other genera in the Vandaceous group into multigeneric hybrids of charm
and vivid color. Flowers are generally smaller, but on long, sometimes
branched inflorescences. Phalaenopsis × Ascocentrum = Asconopsis;
Phalaenopsis × Renanthera = Renanthopsis; Phalaenopsis × Doritis ×
Ascocentrum = Beardara. These are a few of the combinations.

Aerides dominianum has lovely two-foot spikes of rosy lavender and white flowers. This hybrid was made in 1871 by Veitch in England.

Ascocentrum miniatum has one-half inch orange flowers. Ascocentrums are crossed with vandas, which have larger flowers and plants, to make intermediate-sized ascocendas.

Vanda

Abbreviation V. Pronunciation "VAN-duh"

Vandas are warm climate orchids. They love the sun and the rain and the tropical breezes. They have flowers that are rather round, flat and very colorful. Flower sizes range from one-half inch to five inches in diameter each way.

Vandas are monopodial orchids and produce their flowers in upright spikes of several blooms each. Many plants will have multiple spikes at one time, some bloom repeatedly so they are almost constantly in flower.

Vandas are divided into three groups according to leaf character.

TERETE VANDAS — Terete means "circular" or "cylindrical" and teretes are easy to recognize because the leaves and the main stem are round like pencils. Pronunciation "teh-REET."

The most famous of this group is Vanda Miss Joaquim, whose lavender flowers used for leis are grown by the acre and sold by the pound in Hawaii, and grown for hedges in Singapore, where it originated, and other tropical areas. Vanda teres and V. hookeriana are other notable teretes.

Renanthopsis Alice has yellow flowers spotted with red. (Left) Vanda Tatzeri is a free blooming hybrid with flowers in pink, brown and yellow.

Vanda sanderiana (now Euanthe sanderiana) is the parent of many of the strapleaf vanda hybrids.

STRAPLEAF VANDAS — The term strapleaf describes the vandas in this category because they have long, narrow leaves. Leaves run about one and one-half inches wide and twelve or more inches long. They arch from the main stem and are creased along the midrib.

Strapleaf vandas have been hybridized through many generations. The most famous parent is Vanda sanderiana (botanically Euanthe sanderiana), a spectacular species from the Philippines that imparts color, size and form to the flowers of its hybrids. Vanda coerulea, a blue-flowered species, is used for its color. V. Rothschildiana, a hybrid of these two species, is famous for the size, form and color of its round, flat lavender-blue blooms.

SEMI-TERETE VANDAS — A third classification concerns hybrids between terete and strapleaf vandas, which have progressed through several generations with spectacular flowers. They grow tall, have leaves roundish and grooved, intermediate between the parent types.

Vanda Nellie Morley, a strawberry red, is one of these. V. Tan Chay Yan, with large apricot flowers is another. There are many attractive hybrids in this group.

ASCOCENTRUM — Abbreviation Asctm. Pronunciation "ass-koh-SEN-trum."

This genera fits in here because Ascocentrum has been hybridized with Vanda to make Ascocenda which is designed to miniaturize the plants and flowers. Hybridizing has advanced so far that some of the blooms are as large as those of vandas, but on more manageable plants. The hybrids are lovely and take less space than vandas.

J. Nugent. Fitch del et lith.   R. S. Williams & Son Publ's.

VANDA TERES ANDERSONI

Christieara Malibu Gold is a trigeneric hybrid of Vanda, Aerides and Ascocentrum.

Ascocentrum plants are small, the thick leaves not more than 10 inches long. Flower spikes are six to eight inches high with many bright orange, rose or scarlet round, flat flowers less than an inch in diameter. Asctm. curvifolium is the species most used in hybridization, with such famous offspring as Ascocenda Yip Sum Wah, Ascda. Ophelia and the like.

Ascocentrums are monopodial orchids native from the Himalayas through southeast Asia and are grown like vandas.

CULTURE — Vandas mostly originate in the warm climates of southeast Asia with the exception of the blue Vanda coerulea and a few others which grow in cool, high altitude areas. The species may bloom at set seasons, but the hybrids may flower repeatedly.

Vandas like sunlight and exposed situations, the teretes need brighter light than the strapleaves, and all need warm moist, moving air. If your climate is suitable, put the vandas outdoors when the temperature is above about 65°F, in the sun, rain and wind. Vandas are not suitable for houseplants, nor for climates with dark and short days.

Vandas may be grown in baskets, pots or on slabs or totems. Most of the roots will avoid the container and hang out in the air. Any potting medium must be porous and drain rapidly.

Fertilizing can be generous providing there is bright light, moisture and high temperature. All these factors must be in balance. Vandas are very durable plants, and can use lots of light. However, they can sunburn if moved suddenly into a brighter location, so changes should be gradual.

Other Vandaceous Orchids

Several other genera of monopodials related to vandas are well worth growing if your conditions permit.

ARACHNIS (Arach.) — Bizarre "spider orchids" need strong sunlight and are suitable to tropical locations. They grow to 10 feet or more in height.

AERIDES (Aer.) — These plants are smaller in stature than the rampant strapleaf vandas, have pendant inflorescences with closely spaced flowers mostly with white and rose-purple blooms. They grow in less light than the strapleaf vandas.

RENANTHERA (Ren.) — Renantheras are long-legged plants with long, branched spikes of brilliant reddish-orange blooms with spots. The blooms have narrow segments with space between all sepals and petals. They must have bright sun for several hours per day. Renantheras have been crossed with many other genera and the hybrids are very attractive.

RHYNCHOSTYLIS (Rhy.) — Called "foxtail orchids" because of the pendant spikes crowded with less than one-inch flowers. Flowers are white with amethyst spots. The monopodial plants are short with about three or four pairs of leaves, and grow well in hanging baskets.

MULTIGENERICS — All of the above, plus other vandaceous orchids have been crossed to make colorful and floriferous hybrids, many of which deserve to be in a collection if conditions are suitable. They are easy to grow and generous in flower production.

Paphiopedilum Mary Noble.

Paphioipedilum/Slipper Orchids

Abbreviation Paph. Pronunciation "paff-ee-oh-PED-il-um."

The tropical slipper orchids from southeast Asia are very exotic. They are small plants which don't take up much space and are attractive for their foliage even when not in flower. The blooms may last several weeks under normal conditions. They come in interesting colors and artistic patterns.

The plants are sympodial but without bulbs with about six leaves per division, leaves that may be one to three inches wide and three to 16 inches long. The normal range is about six inches long. Leaves are placed close together on the central core, and the divisions are connected by a rhizome that is almost non-existent, one-fourth inch at most, but usually the growths are right next to each other. New growths come from between the lower leaves of the mature growths. Flower spikes rise from the very center of the fan of leaves after the growth is mature.

Paphiopedilum Clairvoyance is a bulldog type of fine form.

87

For a century the books have said that the mottled-leaved types were "warm-growing" and that the plain-leaved types were "cool-growing," and they would not grow well together. Also that paphs like coolness and shade. In our experience, none of this is exactly true.

Here in Jacksonville, Florida, we grow paphs with plain leaves and paphs with mottled leaves side by side in a greenhouse with all our other orchids — cattleyas, phalaenopsis, vandas and others. The only concession we make is to put the plain-leaved types at the end of the greenhouse near the coolers, and the mottled leaves a few feet away. All get bright light, which is balanced with high humidity, frequent watering, moving air and fertilizer every week when supplied to all the other plants. The greenhouse is only 15 x 32 feet.

Paphiopedilums are terrestrial plants that grow in humus on the ground, but some are found in tree crotches or rock crevices where humus collects. They need a potting medium that holds water without becoming soggy. Every paph grower has his favorite mix. We use seedling bark, tree fern, charcoal bits, perlite chips, shredded sphagnum moss with some additions of bonemeal, superphosphate, perhaps rotted cow manure. When the mix deteriorates so that some roots are showing we put on a top layer of homemade compost (well-rotted oak leaves, grass clippings, kitchen vegetable trimmings, etc.).

The best advice to beginners is to buy potting mix where you buy your plants.

The flower parts of the slipper orchids are quite different from those of other orchid flowers because the basic structure is modified. See sketches in Chapter I. The lip is the slipper. The other two petals are generally held horizontally but hang down if they are very long. The dominant dorsal sepal at the top is broader than the petals, rounded with a pointed tip. The other two sepals are fused into one small segment which may be hidden behind the pouch. This segment is called a synsepalum. The column at the center of the flower and just above the pouch is flat, usually round, and called a staminode.

Flowers may be produced singly, in pairs, or several in succession in the group called multifloras.

Paphs have been cultivated since the beginning of orchid growing in Europe and many hybrids have been made. The advanced hybrids with large, round flowers are called "bulldogs."

The genus name comes from Greek words meaning "Venus" and "sandal."

PHRAGMIPEDIUM — Abbreviation Phrag. Pronunciation "frag-mih-PEE-dee-um."

This genus of slipper orchids is native to the Western Hemisphere from Guatemala across the entire top half of South America. There are about

Paphiopedilum Saint Swithin is a primary hybrid of the multiflora type. Parents are Paph. philippinense x Paph. rothschildianum. This hybrid, made in 1901, is still a favored plant of today's growers because of the striking flowers of creamy yellow-green with chocolate markings. It wins many awards.

Paphiopedilum godefroyae is a handsome species from S. Vietnam, Thailand and Burma where it grows on limestone. The flowers are white or cream, heavily spotted with magenta.

Phragmipedium caudatum has pale green and pink flowers, the petals more than a foot long. Phragmipediums are native to Central and South America.

a dozen species, some with very large leaves and foot-high spikes that have many blooms opening in succession. The flowers are distinguished from the paphs in that the petals are unusually long, narrow and sometimes twisted, the dorsal sepal is not very wide, and the synsepalum may be larger than paph types. Culture as for paphiopedilums.

SELENIPEDIUM — Terrestrial plants of large size and small flowers, native from Costa Rica into Colombia and Brazil. There are only four species, not much grown in cultivation.

CYPRIPEDIUM — Pronounced "sip-ree-PEE-dee-um."

Until recently the species now classed as Paphiopedilum were listed as Cypripedium and show up that way in the early hybrid lists and old books. Now the genus Cypripedium is limited to the slipper orchids of the North Temperate Zone and the U.S. native slippers are in this group.

There are about 20 to 30 species spread over temperate climates in North America, Europe and Asia. These are terrestrial plants that do not take kindly to garden cultivation.

Of the North American slippers the best known is Cypripedium acaule, the "pink moccasin-flower", which grows from the Arctic Circle across central and eastern Canada, around the Great Lakes, and south into North Carolina. The "yellow moccasin-flower", Cypripedium calceolus grows in Europe and North America.

The "pink moccasin flower," Cypripedium acaule is a North American slipper orchid. It is terrestrial and grows in high, dry woodlands in shifting shade. This one flowered on the Eastern Shore of Maryland in the spring.

Dendrobium

Abbreviation Den. Pronunciation: "den-DROH-bee-um."

Dendrobiums are very popular in many countries because of the variety of their blooms, definite growth patterns and floriferousness.

Some dendrobiums are evergreen, some are deciduous, some are called cane orchids because the pseudobulbs are tall and thin. All are sympodial.

This is an enormous genus with perhaps more than 1,000 species. Some are monsters and some are miniatures. There are thousands of hybrids.

Dendrobiums are native in the high Himalayas and mountainsides in Japan through the hot areas of southeast Asia and Indonesia and down the entire east side of Australia.

Since some of the species are native at sea level and some at high elevations, they have varying habits. As a general rule, the dendrobiums grow during the summer or wet season and flower during the dry or cool season. If plants take a definite rest, less water and lower temperatures are necessary.

Most grow best in very small pots or on slabs so they dry off quickly, and good air circulation is important. So is bright light, as many of them need several hours of high light intensity to grow and bloom. Some need a chilling period before blooming.

Some flowers are fleeting, but some last for several weeks and cut sprays of dendrobiums are more and more available in the florist market.

Because dendrobiums are so varied you could make a whole collection of them and have lovely and different flowers almost around the calendar.

Dendrobium Autumn Lace 'Florida Twist' is a mericlone of a dwarf strain of antelope dendrobium. Other antelopes may make canes six feet tall.

DENDROBIUM NOBILE — These plants make soft canes about a foot high with leaves along the lengths. They are very popular in cultivation, especially the advanced hybrids in many colors. They grow rapidly during the summer if given bright sun, small pots, lots of water and fertilizer. They must have moving air to stand the bright light. They need at least a month of dryness and chilling down almost to freezing. Fertilizer containing nitrogen should be withheld when the canes are mature. Then when taken into a warmer area, the buds begin to form along the stems and the plants are in glorious bloom during February, March and April with flowers in pairs, from nodes along the stems. Blooms come on new and old bulbs.

DENDROBIUM PHALAENOPSIS — The species name is confusing because it is the same as the genus Phalaenopsis. The plants are no kin, but the flowers of these dendrobiums have a shape similar to phalaenopsis.

These are stiff cane types with leaves at the top. They grow rapidly during the summer with encouragement, and flower in the fall. Blooms come

In Bangkok, Thailand, Dendrobium phalaenopsis are grown for cut flowers. Here hundreds of plants are suspended under bamboo lath over a klong. They go to the floating market by boat.

93

on long spikes produced at the top of old and new canes. Colors range in the hybrids from pure white to deepest magenta. These plants don't need to be chilled. They grow by the millions in Bangkok, Thailand, where the weather is always hot.

EVERGREEN DENDROBIUMS — This group includes a vast number of hybrids derived from crossings of Den. stratoites, Den. gouldii and others with tall, erect canes that may be three feet or more in height. Flower spikes are long and long-lasting. Some blooms have upright, narrow and twisted petals like horns, which give them the name "antelope orchids." The flowers are decorative and may be found in the florist trade

OTHER SPECIES — Dendrobium aggregatum has small bulbs and single leaves, together no longer than a person's thumb. Flowers in pendant sprays are round and like showers of golden coins.

Dendrobium speciosum, is called "rock lily" in its native Australia because it grows in exposed situations. It is very hardy and grows in clumps with the stout pseudobulbs crowded close together. It needs fresh air and bright light, and can stand light frost.

Flowers are small, white, cream or yellowish, but produced in great quantities on large plants.

Dendrobium smilliae has flowers so arranged it is called "bottlebrush orchid" and Den. secundum has an inflorescence like a purple toothbrush!

(Left) Dendrobium speciosum grows in huge clumps in its native habitat in eastern Australia. (Right) Dendrobium teretifolium growing on a tree on Fiji. Note length of the circular leaves.

J. Nugent Fitch del et lith.

B.S. Williams & Son Publr⁵

ODONTOGLOSSUM PRIONOPETALUM.

Odontoglossum

Abbreviation: Odm. Pronunciation: "oh-DONT-oh-gloss-um."

No matter what we said about many orchids growing together, the odontoglossums must have cool temperatures. The species from the Colombian Andes, such as Odm. crispum, need protection from extremes in temperature. Wild plants grow in buoyant but damp atmosphere, and in the warmer weather are shaded by overhead foliage, refreshed by frequent showers, and fanned by moving air.

Ideal temperature ranges are in the 50 °F range at night and 60 °F range by day. Light must be indirect, and most importantly, the air must be moving. Water must be frequent and the humidity must be high. Fertilizer during the growing season should be at half-strength and interspersed with applications of clear water.

Growers have their favorite potting mixes, and a beginner should get instructions for repotting from the nurseryman who grew the plants.

Central American species, such as Odm. grande, are easier to grow in warm climate collections, as are some of the bigeneric hybrids such as Odontocidiums (Odm. × Oncidium).

Odontoglossum edwardii, drawing from The Orchid Album.

Miltonias are called "pansy orchids."

Miltonia

Abbreviation: Milt. Pronunciation: "mil-TOH-nee-uh."

Miltonias are called "pansy orchids" bcause of their roundish, flat flowers, but they are much larger than the annual pansies in our gardens.

There are two major groups. The Colombian species and hybrids termed cool-growing and the Brazilian species and hybrids termed warm-growing. All of them prefer cool nights because they come from high elevations in these and neighboring countries and up into Central America.

The Colombian Miltonias are now classified as Miltoniopsis. However, hybrid registrations continue as Miltonia because it would be impossible to untangle past registrations.

The plants have thin, light green leaves which curve gracefully from tops and sides of the pseudobulbs. Adequate light is needed, but more shade is desirable in hot weather to reduce leaf temperature. Moving air and sufficient water are needed to prevent excessive evaporation. In a multi-genera greenhouse, the Brazilian miltonias do best near the coolers.

Miltonias have fine roots and need to be grown in containers that may seem too small so there is no excess medium to stay wet. They need to be damp all the time but never soggy. They do well in shallow baskets of tree fern, but growers use several media. Fertilizer should be half-strength given only during the growing season except for plants in bark which need 30-10-10 all year.

Miltonias come in lovely colors, some solid, some with contrasting masks. Miltonia Anne Warne, a hybrid of the Brazilian Milt. spectabilis, is a famous Hawaiian hybrid that does well in warm climates.

Many bigeneric hybrids of Miltonia with Aspasia, Brassia and Oncidium grow well in warm climates. Multigenerics for cooler climates include Withnerara (Aspasia × Oncidium × Odontoglossum × Miltonia).

Oncidium

Abbreviation: Onc. Pronunciation: "on-SID ce-um."

The delightful "dancing ladies" of the orchid world are the oncidiums. Most of the flowers, vary in size from a fraction to five inches and have large lips like swirling ballet skirts. Many are produced in great numbers on long spikes, some of which branch. The exotic Onc. papilio and related "butterfly orchids" look more like butterflies than flowers.

Yellow and brown are the usual oncidium colors, but the equitants have a wide range of pink and magenta shades as well.

Oncidiums are native to south Florida, the West Indies, Cuba, Jamaica, southern Mexico, Central America, and the whole wide top half of South America.

Most of them grow in any of the usual mixes and containers providing they dry out between waterings. The equitants are very fussy about watering and need special attention.

Many of the oncidiums grow in warm conditions except for a few that come from high altitudes.

This is a large genus of 400 to 500 species. There are roughly four groups:

BULBOUS — These have definite pseudobulbs but the composition varies considerably. They may be round, flat and rough like Onc. ampliatum with its thick, dark green broad leaves, or light green upright ovals like Onc. sphacelatum which has narrow thin ribbon-like leaves.

RATTAIL — Pendulous terete (round) leaves of rattail oncidiums generally indicate that plants grow where conditions are dry. They need to be warm, dry and exposed to bright light. They are best grown on slabs.

MULE EAR — These oncidiums have heavy, wide leaves creased in the center and pointed at the top. Like a mule's ear, if anybody remembers what a mule looks like. They have rather squatty bulbs which range in size as do the leaves. Onc. splendidum is a familiar one of this group. It puts up straight tall spikes of bright yellow dancers.

EQUITANT — These are very small plants with their little leaves (generally two to four inches long) arranged in fans. The little flowers appear on the tops of slender upright spikes that may be a foot high. There are many hybrids in many color patterns in the yellow and red variations.

Equitant oncidiums have flowers about an inch wide in a variety of beautiful color combinations. The plants are very small.

Masdevallia macrura drawn by J. N. Fitch for The Orchid Album.

Culture of oncidiums varies with the group. Many grow in cattleya type conditions along with other orchids, but are inclined to take a resting period. Roots are fine so the potting medium needs to drain quickly.

... And More

The above touch on some of the favorite cultivated orchids, but there are many other fascinating orchids that you will see at shows and in greenhouses. Consider these:

ANGRAECUM — And other genera native to Africa and Madagascar. Angraecums, large and small have white starry flowers because they are pollinated by night-flying moths. These are monopodial plants with flowers from a fraction to seven inches across.

ANSELLIA — The African "leopard orchids" with stiff, upright cylindrical bulbs and yellow and brown spotted flowers.

BULBOPHYLLUM — A huge genus of perhaps 2,000 species, some

plants large and some small, all with curious flowers. They are native in tropical areas around the globe.

LYCASTE — Attractive soft-leaved plants with showy flowers in which the three sepals are very large and the two small lateral petals hug the column. Flower color white, pink, orange, yellow and olive green.

MASDEVALLIA — Cool growing orchids from Central and South America with very distinctive flowers in which the sepals are the showy parts. Brightly colored, they wave like flags atop slender stems rising above the foliage. Leaves are narrow, single, upright. Low light suits masdevallias, and many of the small plants are grown in windowsill collections, but there are large species with 12-inch flowers.

STANHOPEA — These plants must be grown hanging in open baskets or on slabs because the flower spikes hang down from below the bulbs. Flowers are quite distinct and need to be seen to be believed.

Terrestrial Orchids

Many of the native North American orchids are terrestrials. Reference to a wildflower book will show you that many of the flowers on roadsides, bogs or open fields are orchids. To say nothing of spiranthes, which pop up in suburban lawns in early summer.

Our native orchids are usually difficult to grow in cultivation, but terrestrials from other countries are more amenable including Phaius, Calanthe, Spathoglottis and some of the "jewel orchids" with decorative foliage. These terrestrials are attractive in containers on terraces and patios.

Friends decorated the speakers' platform with pots of blooming orchids when Dr. Frances Bartlett Kinne was inaugurated President of Jacksonville University in Florida.

Miniatures in the Cattleya Alliance. (Left) Lc. Memoria Jean Kieman. (Lower left) Cattleytonia Keith Roth. (Right) Kirchara Sundance.

  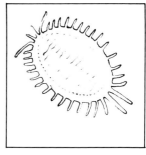

| Aphid | Thrips | Mealybug |

CHAPTER VIII

PROBLEMS

Orchid plants are tough and are not appetizing to many garden pests. But alas, there are some pests who think them delicious.

There are three points of great importance.

1. Identify your problem, then choose a control which takes care of it. If you treat a pest or disease with some chemical to which it does not react, it is a waste of your time and money.

2. Use any product exactly as directed on the label. Read every word of the label before applying. Mix in exact proportions. Apply exactly as specified, noting temperature ranges if, for instance, it advises against application at higher than 80°F, don't apply when the temperature is 85°F. Twice as much is not better, it is worse, as you may damage your plants even if one-third teaspoon to a quart does not seem like much.

3. Take all advised precautions, and then some. Never smoke when using chemicals. All you need is one drop of chemical on a cigarette, inhale it, and you'll regret it. Wear coverup clothes (not shorts and sandals), cover your head, and if necessary, wear gloves and glasses. Don't rub your eyes, eat, drink, smoke or even shake hands with somebody before you bathe and change clothes.

Application is easy now. Some chemicals come in aerosol cans. If the label says hold the can 24 inches from the plant, do so, or the carrier of the insecticide might damage the plant. Some products contain combinations of insecticides and fungicides.

An easy way to manage a small collection is to keep handy a quart bottle with a squirt top, available at any hardware store, and mix an all-purpose insecticide such as malathion in it. Keep this in the greenhouse, and when you see a mealybug or some scale, squirt then and there. Make another bottle for fungicide. Use different colored labels to identify your bottles, tag them with the name of the product and the dilution so your refilling information is right there.

If you don't know how to translate gallons into quarts, or cups into tablespoons, look for conversion tables in a basic cookbook.

We are not giving recommendations by product names because these change too often. If you buy your plants locally, consult your nurseryman. If not, consult your local agricultural agent or state university for recommendations.

The Controls

PESTICIDES are specialized, so choose according to what they control.

INSECTICIDES are for control of insects.

FUNGICIDES are for control of fungus diseases.

MITICIDES are for control of mites, also called spider mites and red spiders. These are not insects but arachnids — and may not respond to insecticides. Baits and dusts are designated for control of snails and slugs, which are not insects either.

Inspect new plants thoroughly before putting them near your other plants. Look for any signs of pests or diseases, and if possible isolate new plants for a few weeks to see if anything turns up. Don't buy bargain plants that look weak, discolored or shriveled. Buy only healthy, vigorous plants.

The Pests

SCALE — The most common and worrisome pest on cattleyas and their allies is Boisduval scale. The insects are white, tiny like pinheads, but in a cluster look like fuzzy white powder. They collect under the brown tissue covering the bulbs and can destroy the dormant eyes so the plant can't grow. They collect in leaves where they fold together on top of the bulbs, on undersides of leaves, and particularly on young seedling plants.

There are brown and red scales like pinheads that may appear singly on any orchid leaves, especially the undersides, on flower spikes of phalaenopsis and other genera.

Scales are sucking insects that cause damaged parts to turn yellow and then black.

Soft white scale is a serious problem on orchids.

Spray with an insecticide, then rub off with a soft toothbrush. Take care not to rub off the eyes of sympodial plants.

MEALYBUGS, APHIDS, THRIPS — Mealybugs are white powdery ovals, some with tails. They are clearly visible but they hide, particularly around flower buds, in the crowns and along the flower stems of paphiopedilums, and tuck themselves in where phalaenopsis buds join the stems.

Thrips are difficult to see and may attack flower buds so the blooms open deformed or discolored. Worse yet, they carry diseases.

Aphids are familiar to every gardener and they attack new growth, causing damage and deformity by sucking plant juices. They multiply rapidly.

SOWBUGS, MILLIPEDES, SPRINGTAILS—Infest the potting mix and do damage to roots. Watch for them when you repot.

ANTS, TERMITES — These familiar pests may nest in the pots and if you notice them coming and going, turn the plant out of the pot and get rid of them and their eggs before repotting.

ROACHES — Roaches love the taste of orchid flowers. If you find blooms that have been chewed overnight, suspect some roaches living in the pots. Roach baits enclosed in plastic traps offer good control. Use any control you use in your house, but don't spray roach poison on plants or pots or potting mixtures, only on benches between pots. Baits are better.

MITES — Mites are sucking pests of the spider family that may be difficult to see, except that an infested leaf may have a reddish tinge underneath like it is sprinkled with red pepper, or a suggestion of fine webs. Mites collect on undersides of soft foliage and must be controlled with special preparations. However, spraying them directly with water is somewhat effective.

SLUGS AND SNAILS — These are chewers that mostly work by night. They may feast on roots, new growths, and especially on flowers. They hide during the day and come out when the temperature falls and moisture rises, so they may be seen on cloudy days.

Bush snails are tiny brown round-shelled creatures that eat roots. Larger snails and slugs from a fraction to several inches long may be inhabiting pots. Look for their slimy trails.

There are good granular baits for snails and slugs that should be put out in the evening on a bottle cap or a piece of crock, not directly on a plant or potting mix. Another way is to put lettuce leaves on the pot surfaces at dusk, inspect them in a few hours after dark and remove any slugs or snails.

The Diseases

Diseases are difficult to diagnose in plants, and virus is as mysterious in plants as it is in people.

Strong, healthy plants that are well grown will have fewer problems than neglected, crowded plants that are weak and invite infections.

ROTS are often caused by collection of moisture in plant crowns, leaf crevices, and new leads, especially in low temperatures. One way to reduce the risk is to water plants early in the day when the weather is cold so the foliage dries off before night. Bacterial brown spot on phalaenopsis is a serious problem as it can begin anywhere on a leaf and spread rapidly. If it reaches the crown of the plant, the plant is doomed.

VIRUS DISEASES cannot be detected, only suspected, without scientific tests which your state university or agricultural department may perform for you on suspect plants. Discolored foliage and flowers are symptoms, but these may be caused by other diseases, pests or environmental conditions. Cymbidium mosaic virus is not limited to cymbidiums.

PETAL BLIGHT (Botrytis) forms dark pinpoint spots on flowers in cool weather. Lack of air circulation contributes to its development.

FUNGUS DISEASES spot leaves and flowers. These include the rusts which are orange.

TREATMENT — If possible, get the disease identified. One first step is to cut off (with sterilized tools) any infected portion of a plant back to good green tissue. Then drench with a fungicide or bactericide in the recommended proportion. Avoid splashing water on plants, as it may spread the disease to other plants.

In a small collection, a quart spray-top bottle of fungicide can be used at the first sign of a problem, as recommended earlier in this chapter.

Environmental Problems

Too much water or not enough water may cause roots to deteriorate (the former more than the latter), and plants to die without real symptoms.

Slug is a night prowler. Rainfrog is a friend.

Uncongenial temperatures, air pollution, insufficient light, too much dry air, too much fertilizer, or pesticide too strong, may cause plants to decline or die. The elements of culture must be balanced to promote good health and strong growth.

Sanitation

Keep your greenhouse clean. Remove fallen leaves and other debris, cut off wilted flowers. Keep a garbage can lined with a plastic bag in the greenhouse and drop debris in it. Keep covered with a lid. Put bag and all out for garbage collection. Don't put this type of debris on your compost pile.

Sterilization of tools is important to cut down spread of disease, which can be transferred from one plant to another by the sap that sticks to the cutting instrument.

A very easy way to sterilize your tools is to soak them in a solution of trisodium phosphate. This is a white powder cleaner available at any hardware store.

Have a glass jar with a wide mouth and a tight lid, the opening wide enough to accommodate the handles of your scissors, clippers and other tools. Fill the jar with enough water to cover the cutting surfaces of the tools, but not necessarily the handles. Do not use an aluminum container.

Drop enough trisodium phosphate into the water that it does not all dissolve when stirred. The water should be at room temperature, or about 70°F. The solution should be slightly milky.

Soak tools at least five minutes before using on another plant, longer is better. Keep jar covered when tools are not in use so the air does not counteract the alkalinity of the phosphate solution.

Pour out the old solution and remix it fresh when it becomes dirty from debris, evaporates below the original level, or when it ceases to feel soapy.

Pots should be thoroughly washed after use, then soaked in a fresh 2% Clorox solution and rinsed before use. Scrub pot clips and stakes also.

Friends

If you grow orchids in a warm climate, you have some very helpful garden and greenhouse friends to help you eradicate pests you will never see. Chameleons eat insects all day long, toads hop around housekeeping under the benches, and little green rainfrogs move from plant to plant and sing little songs. Encourage your friends and watch out for them if you are spraying with pesticides.

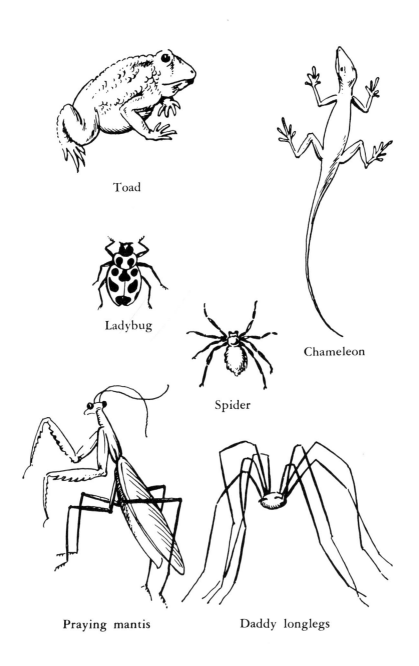

Toad

Ladybug

Spider

Chameleon

Praying mantis

Daddy longlegs

Many garden and greenhouse friends provide efficient day and night pest control services at no charge.

Green orchids. (Top) Coelogyne Burfordiense has lime green sepals and petals. The lip is marked with black. (Left) Angraecum eburneum var. longicalcar has waxy flowers of jade and ivory with long nectary spurs.

CHAPTER IX

HOUSING

A beautiful big greenhouse is the dream of every orchid grower. Yet the majority of hobbyists are growing orchids without expensive equipment. The better conditions you offer, the better your plants will grow, but the secret is to do the best you can with what you have.

However, automatic equipment can save you time from routine chores and leave more time for more enjoyable aspects of orchid growing.

People grow orchids in large and small home greenhouses, in kitchen and bathroom windows, in bay windows, family rooms, glass enclosed porches, in high rise condominiums, in apartments, basements, attics and on balconies.

Greenhouses

The easiest way to control the environment for an orchid collection is in a greenhouse. Many genera of orchids can be grown together, and you can achieve this even in a small house by growing phalaenopsis in the shady part, hanging vandas from the rafters, the cattleyas in bright situations and the paphiopedilums near the coolers.

The size of the house depends upon space available in the yard, the number of plants you wish to have and can take care of. No matter how big you build it, the greenhouse will fill up fast.

A greenhouse offers endless pleasure because you can work with your plants at night, during bad weather or on dreary winter evenings.

Even in warm climates a greenhouse is good for plants, especially if it has cooling and humidifying equipment. It permits you to control the amount of light, shade, water, wind, temperature and humidity.

There are a great many attractive prefabricated greenhouses on the market in free-standing and lean-to designs. Send for catalogs and study them. It is cheaper in the long run to erect a professionally designed house than to build your own. The prefab design has such important things as drip grooves to carry off the condensation of moisture, and the right slant to the roof for the most light. The materials are impervious to weather

A greenhouse with high sides and a high ridge has space inside for air to move above the plants.

Orchids like to hang up near the glass. Equipment photo shows gas heater and tank, evaporative cooler.

and moisture. If you build your own you may find that it leaks, drips and rots and is expensive to keep in repair.

An important point — if you build your greenhouse or the benches in it, do not use lumber treated with creosote. Some orchids react to fumes from treated wood. Redwood and cypress are the best choices.

Consider these points when studying greenhouse catalogs:

Size. If the greenhouse comes in sections you can add to it later if you have yard space, but it is easier to build as big as you can afford in the beginning.

Glass or plastic? Both have advantages, but some plastics turn dark or brittle with age, so glass would be cheaper because it would not need to be replaced. Plastic sheeting is too fragile, as a windstorm can damage it. If your climate is warm, a plastic house may get too hot unless you have adequate ventilation and cooling equipment.

Another point is climate. If you live in a cold climate, choose a design that has low sidewalls and a slant to the roof sufficient so snow slides off. But if your climate is warm much of the year and hot in the summer, you need a style with high side walls which raise the roof well above the plants. This allows for a cushion of air over the plants, tempers fast outside temperature changes, and allows for better air circulation. You need

(Opposite page) Many of our orchids hang outdoors on the patio during warm weather. We can enjoy the blooms from inside our family room. (This page) View before we covered the patio. What the neighbors see.

Lath shade on a penthouse terrace garden makes a good place to grow orchids.

to have your roof high enough so you can hang plants above those on the benches. With some prefab models it is well to increase the foundation by another row or two of concrete blocks. This gives much more inside greenhouse space.

Adequate ventilation is most important. Hot air rises, and in any climate there must be openings in the top of the roof to let the hot air escape.

Large panes of glass are more resilient than small panes and less likely to break if something falls on them.

Choice of heating equipment depends on the size of the house and the cost of fuels available to you. Special greenhouse heaters are built to withstand the humid atmosphere better than home heaters. Any heating system should be controlled by a thermostat because weather can change suddenly in the middle of the night or when you are not at home.

Cooling in hot weather is desirable. Home air conditioners take moisture out of the air, so a greenhouse cooler should be of the wet-pad type that puts moisture into the air. A ceiling fan (preferably a greenhouse turbulator) to circulate the air at all times is helpful. Orchids are air plants and dislike a stuffy atmosphere.

Shading in summer is necessary in almost every climate. Shade paint may be applied to glass with a paint sprayer or rollers. Greenhouse type paint is available from greenhouse companies.

Where to locate your greenhouse is important. Remember that plants need morning sun all year, so east or south exposures are best. You can add shade but not light. However, nearby trees which provide moving shade patterns over the greenhouse can be very helpful in providing a congenial atmosphere. If shade is dense, don't cut down a tree, just thin out some of the branches so more light comes through.

Benches for orchids should be open rather than solid, preferably made of pressed steel or hardware cloth. Be sure bench legs are termite and rot proof but not creosoted. Tiered benches give more shelf space than flat benches and make plants easier to care for because those on the back row are more visible and accessible. Prefab wire benches are good choices.

Orchids Outdoors

Where the climate is suitable, orchids are good for landscaping. They can be grown on live trees, driftwood trees, tree fern poles, in pots and baskets. Great beds of reed-stem epidendrums and semi-terete and terete vandas can landscape whole tropical gardens.

Indoor-outdoor arrangements are useful where the climate is not warm enough for orchids to stay outdoors all year. Hanging pots, baskets or slabs from trees, a trellis, a patio cover, or setting pots in locations of suitable light, can provide decoration in good growing conditions.

At our home in northeast Florida we have a patio covered with saran screen over white wood supports, with chains along the house eaves on one side and the edge of the trellis on the other. Vandas, ascocendas and other plants in bloom enhance the view from our family room all during warm weather. We also have plant stands with overhead covers in the back of the garden, where growing conditions are ideal for six or eight months per year, and plants from there are moved into the display patio when in bloom. All plants go into the greenhouse in winter.

High rise terraces may be too windy for orchids. If the terrace is big enough it can support a small greenhouse. Another alternative is a lath structure to temper the wind and sun.

Orchids Indoors

Many people grow orchids in their homes. The temperature is about right except that humidity is too low. Using your brightest east or south window for a growing area may provide enough light. Humidity can be increased by setting the pots on pebbles in trays filled with water so organized that pots are above, not in, the water.

A bay window in a house makes a good plant area with light from three sides. Remember how grandma grew ferns in the bay window?

Prefab window greenhouses are attractive additions, and now come both higher and wider than the actual window opening. Some new houses have large picture-windows which extend out from the wall, with a built-in waterproof base for display of plants, orchids, foliage or other flowering potted plants. This type window should face north since it is for display, not growing, and needs to be in the shade.

Artificial light is the only kind of light some orchids see if grown indoors.

There are high quality plant lights available that combine the elements of the light spectrum to provide for growth and flowering. The height of the lights above the plants is a factor which must be worked out. An easy way to begin is with a commercial plant cart that has several tiers of waterproof shelves with lights above.

Many orchids set buds according to daylength. Some need short days and some need long days. This will influence your choices of plants to grow. But even a table lamp that burns late at night nearby might upset the timing.

Plant size is another factor, as obviously the tall growing monopodials would be awkward, but at the same time the light-loving plants might be difficult to supply with enough light.

Temperature regulation must provide a congenial range for the plants, and the drop at night is extremely important. This might be difficult to do if you keep your home thermostat at 72°F all the time.

Humidity and air movement are also considerations.

All of the above is not intended to scare you off from growing orchids under lights. You need to re-read the earlier chapter on culture to evaluate the factors of good growing, and get them into balance. Many people are successful with orchids indoors under lights. There are articles in the orchid magazines based on personal experiences, and it can be done.

Ansellia ("leopard orchid") grows on a deciduous tree in Mala Mala Game Reserve in Africa.

CHAPTER X

ENJOY AND SHARE

Enjoy your orchids!

Wear them proudly on any occasion. Use them as cut flowers in your home, even on the breakfast table. Bring flowering plants indoors. Set the pots inside decorative cachepots or display plans right in their own pots without covers. This is perfectly acceptable, and plants are shown like this in the most fashionable magazines. Use plants in your daily living or on special occasions.

Buy a supply of inexpensive bud vases or use small green Perrier water bottles (with labels washed off) to carry single flowers or sprays to hospital patients, shut-ins or people with problems. Or to somebody who is giving a party. You don't need foliage or a fancy design.

Take orchids to your office to cheer your co-workers or your boss; to congratulate somebody on a promotion, a birthday, or a new baby. Share your flowers with a bereaved family or a happy family.

Set pots of blooming orchids across the front of a speaker's platform on a special occasion.

You will be amazed at how many people have never had an orchid, and you will get a thrill from being the giver of the first one. Any orchids, large or small, convey your message in a very personal way.

Corsages

With all the colors, shapes and sizes available in orchid flowers, there is something for every costume and occasion. Do not make elaborate corsages nor overdress your orchids with so much ribbon that you don't know where the flowers begin. Flowers should dominate.

The first step is to pick the flowers at the proper time. Most orchids open slowly, and flowers that are cut when still green will fold up fast. Cymbidiums should be open on the spike for about 10 days before being cut. Cattleyas take four or five days from the time the buds crack until they should be cut.

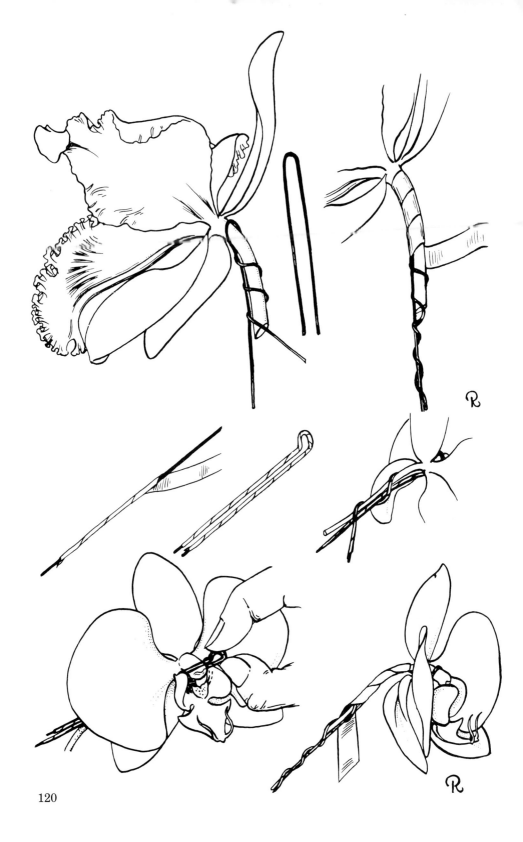

Cut the stem with a sharp knife in a slanting cut. Do not use scissors, which pinch the cells together so stems can't absorb water. Put flowers in water overnight in a cool place away from drafts. About 50 °F is right. Flowers conditioned for about 12 hours should hold up several days without more water.

When you are not wearing a corsage, put it on shredded paper in a covered box and put in the refrigerator.

HOW TO MAKE A CORSAGE — The first step is to wire and tape the stem with florist's supplies, often available in craft shops. Next assemble flowers into a design. Then add ribbon or whatever.

The purpose of wiring is to secure the stem so it doesn't break, and to substitute wire for a bulky stem. Tape hides the wire and protects clothing from wire ends.

Many orchids can be wired by one method. Reduce the stem to one inch or less. Choose wire heavy enough to support but not break the stem. Bend wire through the middle like a hairpin. Put one side against the stem with the hairpin curve right up against the back of the flower at the base of the dorsal sepal. Wrap the other half of the wire below the curve, around the stem and the parallel wire.

For small flowers, use a fine florist's wire, but cover each tiny stem with a piece of tape before wiring and again afterwards.

To tape a flower that has been wired, select floral tape that blends with the bloom. Place one end up at the top of the stem at the back of the flower. Stretching as you go, wrap it around and around to cover the stem and the wires to the bottom. It sticks to itself.

If using more than one flower, wire and tape all of them first, then assemble into the design and fasten them together at one or more points with wire and then tape.

To make a simple bow, fold one loop at a time and pinch across the ribbon with your fingers as you put the loop in place. When you have as many loops as you wish, cut a piece of ribbon about eight inches long. Still holding the loops in one hand, twist the new piece through the middle and tie it around the middle of your bow. Tie tightly. The twisting process makes the bow fluffy instead of flat.

Please place flowers right side up in any kind of design.

A boutonniere for a man need only have a short piece of wire and then the stem and wire covered with tape. Be sure to provide a pin as many jackets are made without lapel buttonholes.

Arrangements

Orchids are beautiful in arrangements. They lend themselves to simple or elaborate designs. You can make a Victorian bouquet if you have lots of blooms, or an austere Ikebana arrangement with a few flowers and twigs.

Because stems on individual blooms may be short, you may need to use stakes, tubes or other mechanical aids.

Many people do not know how to arrange orchids because they don't know how they grow and sometimes show them upside down.

If you are not adept at arranging, try simple designs for a mixed vase or a single flower in a bud vase. One trick is to use several different orchids in a series of bud vases set on a flat mirror for a table centerpiece.

Just enjoy your orchids in any way that pleases you.

Two native U.S. orchids. The "eyelash orchid" grows in wet meadows and on roadsides in the Southeastern states. Spiranthes often appear in suburban lawns uninvited.

GENUS NAMES

Hybrids between genera can be distinguished by the combination of names in bigeneric hybrids, those containing two genera: Laeliocattleya = Laelia x Cattleya.

Trigeneric hybrids with three genera in their ancestry may be named with a combination of genera: Sophrolaeliocattleya = Sophronitis x Laelia x Cattleya. Or, trigeneric hybrids may be named as four or more genera in complex hybrids, must be, by the name of an eminent orchidist plus the ending "ara.": Nobleara = Aerides x Renanthera x Vanda; Potinara = Brassavola x Cattleya x Laelia x Sophronitis.

The following are samples of popular genera. Consult Sander's Hybrid Lists for more complete listings.

AERIDES (Aer.) = Natural Genus
AERIDOVANDA (Aerdv.) = Aerides x Vanda
ASCOCENDA (Ascda.) = Ascocentrum x Vanda
ASCOCENTRUM (Asctm.) = Natural genus
BRASSOCATTLEYA (Bc.) = Brassavola x Cattleya
BRASSOEPIDENDRUM (Bepi.) = Brassavola x Epidendrum
BRASSOLAELIOCATTLEYA (Blc.) = Brassavola x Cattleya x Laelia
CATTLEYA (C.) = Natural genus
CYMBIDIUM (Cym.) = Natural genus
DENDROBIUM (Den.) = Natural genus
DIALAELIOCATTLEYA (Dialc.) = Cattleya x Diacrium x Laelia
DORITAENOPSIS (Dtps.) = Doritis x Phalaenopsis
DORITIS (Dor.) = Natural genus
EPICATTLEYA (Epc.) = Cattleya x Epidendrum
EPIDENDRUM (Epi.) = Natural genus
LAELIA (L.) = Natural genus
LAELIOCATONIA (Lctna.) = Broughtonia x Cattleya x Laelia
LAELIOCATTLEYA (Lc.) = Cattleya x Laelia
MACLELLANARA (Mclna.) = Brassia x Odontoglossum x Oncidium
MILTASSIA (Mtssa.) = Brassia x Miltonia
MILTONIDIUM (Mtdm.) = Miltonia x Oncidium
ODONTIODA (Oda.) = Cochlioda x Odontoglossum
ODONTOCIDIUM (Odcdm.) = Odontoglossum x Oncidium
ODONTOGLOSSUM (Odm.) = Natural genus
POTINARA (Pot.) = Brassavola x Cattleya x Laelia x Sophronitis
RENANCENTRUM (Rnctm.) = Ascocentrum x Renanthera
RENANTANDA (Rntda.) = Renanthera x Vanda
RENANTHERA (Ren.) = Natural genus
ROTHARA (Roth.) = Brassavola x Cattleya x Epidendrum x Laelia x Sophronitis
SOPHROLAELIOCATTLEYA (Slc.) = Cattleya x Laelia x Sophronitis
SOPHRONITIS (Soph.) = Natural genus
VANDA (V.) = Natural genus
VANDAENOPSIS (Vdnps.) = Phalaenopsis x Vanda
YAMADARA (Yam.) = Brassavola x Cattleya x Epidendrum x Laelia

THE LANGUAGE OF ORCHIDS

A glossary of some of the words used in this book as they pertain to orchids.

AGAR — Nutrient jelly on which orchid seeds are planted in bottles (flasks).

AWARD — Recognition by an organization.

BACK BULBS — Rear, old pseudobulbs of a sympodial orchid plant. May be cut off and grown into a separate plant if a green eye is present.

BACTERICIDE — Chemical to combat bacterial disease.

BARK — Potting material of dried tree bark.

BIFOLIATE — Plant with two leaves per pseudobulb.

BIGENERIC — Hybrid with two genera in its parentage.

BULB — Pseudobulb. Not a true bulb. A stem for storage of water.

CHLOROPHYLL — Green pigment in plant tissue capable of absorbing light.

CLONE — Individual plant and all of its vegetative divisions.

COLUMN — Structure formed by the combined sexual parts of an orchid flower.

COMMUNITY POT — Group of identical small plants growing in one container.

CROCK — Pieces of broken flower pots, pebbles or other objects placed in the bottom of a container to facilitate drainage.

CROSS — (Verb) Transfer of pollen from one flower to another. (Noun) Hybrid from seed of two unlike parents.

CULTIVAR — Cultivated variety. A single plant and its vegetative propagations.

CULTURE — How to grow.

DIVISION — Piece of a plant. Vegetative propagation.

DORSAL — Dorsal sepal is at the top of the flower.

EPIPHYTE — Air plant which perches on surface of another plant but takes no nourishment from it.

EPITHET — Word or phrase describing a characteristic or quality.

EYE — Embryonic growth bud.

FIR BARK — Potting material.

FLASK — Bottle in which orchid seeds are germinated. (Verb) To sow seeds in bottle on agar.

FUNGICIDE — Chemical for control of fungus disease.

GENERA, GENUS — A group of closely related species (singular). Plural is genera.

GERMINATION — A phase of plant development in which an individual emerges from an embryo or seed.

GREX — "Herd" or "flock." A hybrid name (Grex epithet). Assemblage of all plants with the same hybrid name.

HABITAT — Environment or site in which the population of a certain plant grows wild.

HAPUU — Tree fern fiber for potting.

HUMIDITY — Water vapor content of the atmosphere.

HYBRID — Plant with unlike parents.

INFLORESCENCE — Flowering part of a plant.

INSECTICIDE — Chemical for killing insects.

KEIKI — Offset, adventitious plantlet. New plant produced on old plant, a vegetative offshoot.

LABELLUM — One petal different from the other two. Called "lip" on orchid flower.

LATERAL — From the sides. Applies to the two lower sepals.

LEACH — Wash out with water, as flushing containers with clear water.

LEAD — New growth on a sympodial plant.

LIP — Labellum. The one different petal.

LITHOPHYTE — Plant that grows on rock.

124

MEDIUM — Material in which an orchid is grown in cultivation.

MERICLONE — Plant propagated from a piece of tissue.

MERISTEM — Tissue at the growing point of a plant. A plant propagated from meristem tissue. A mericlone. (Verb) To propagate plants from the meristem tissue.

MONOPODIAL — Plant that grows upward.

MULTIGENERIC — Plant having more than two genera in its ancestry.

NECTARY — Gland in the flower which secretes sugar substance (nectar) which attracts pollinators.

NUTRIENTS — Raw materials in soluble form important to plant growth.

OFFSET — New plant that develops vegetatively on mother plant.

OSMUNDA — Fern root used for potting medium.

OVARY — Part of the flower which develops into the seed pod (fruit).

PEDICEL — Stalk of individual flower.

PETAL — Flower part. Three petals on an orchid, one modified and called lip.

pH — Measure of acidity or alkalinity.

PHOTOSYNTHESIS — Process by which green plants manufacture sugar.

POLLEN, POLLINIUM, POLLINIA — Powder or grains. Male element in fertilization.

PROPAGATE — To multiply.

PROTOCORM — Mass of green cells not yet differentiated into plant parts.

PSEUDOBULB — Thickened stem of an orchid plant. Not a true bulb.

RESPIRATION — Process which releases carbon dioxide and water formed by oxidation.

RHIZOME — Connecting link between pseudobulbs on sympodial plants. A horizontal stem.

RUPICULOUS — Growing on rock.

SEEDLING — Plant grown from seed younger than flowering size or blooming for the first time.

SELF, SELFED, SELFING — Self-fertilization of a flower by its own pollen or that of another flower of the same clone.

SEMI-TERETE — Vanda hybrid with both strapleaf and terete-leaf types in its ancestry.

SEPAL — Outer segments of the flower, three of them.

SHEATH — Protective envelope that encloses emerging buds on some genera.

SPECIES — A group of plants in a genus that are all alike. The word is both singular and plural. "A species." "Several species." Do not say "A specie."

STRAPLEAF — Long, narrow leaves.

SYMPODIAL — A plant that grows sideways with repetitious vertical growths connected by a horizontal stem.

TERETE — Round. Applies to foliage of some orchids.

TERRESTRIAL — Plants that grow in soil.

TREE FERN — Fiber of tropical plant used as a planting medium for orchids.

UNIFOLIATE — Having one leaf per pseudobulb.

VARIETY — A species with some characteristic different from typical form.

VEGETATIVE PROPAGATION — Multiplication without sex, not from seed. See division, back bulb, mericlone, offset.

INDEX

INDEX